Essentials of Advanced Macroeconomic Theory

Trying to summarize the essentials of macroeconomic theory, in the wake of the financial crisis that has shaken not only Western economies but also the macroeconomic profession, is no easy task. In particular, the notion that markets are self-correcting and always in equilibrium appears to have taken a heavy blow. However, the jury is still out on which areas should be considered as failures and which constitute the future of research.

The overall aim of this text is to provide a compact overview of the contributions that are currently regarded as the most important for macroeconomic analysis and to equip the reader with the essential theoretical knowledge that all master's degree students in macroeconomics should be acquainted with.

The result is a compact text that should act as the perfect complement to further study of macroeconomics: an introduction to the key concepts discussed in the journal literature, and suitable for students from upper undergraduate level through to PhD courses.

Ola Olsson is Professor in the Department of Economics at the University of Gothenburg, Sweden.

Routledge Advanced Texts in Economics and Finance

Essentials of Advanced Macroeconomic Theory

Ola Olsson

Routledge
Taylor & Francis Group

LONDON AND NEW YORK

First published 2012
by Routledge
2 Park Square, Milton Park, Abingdon, Oxon OX14 4RN

Simultaneously published in the USA and Canada
by Routledge
711 Third Avenue, New York, NY 10017

Routledge is an imprint of the Taylor & Francis Group, an Informa business

British Library Cataloguing in Publication Data
A catalogue record for this book is available from the British Library

Library of Congress Cataloging in Publication Data
A catalog record for this book has been requested

ISBN: 978-0-415-68505-4 (hbk)
ISBN: 978-0-415-68508-5 (pbk)
ISBN: 978-0-203-13993-6 (ebk)

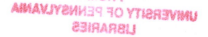

Typeset in Times New Roman by Sunrise Setting Ltd, Torquay, UK.

MIX
Paper from
responsible sources
FSC
www.fsc.org
FSC® C004839

Printed and bound in Great Britain by the MPG Books Group

Contents

List of figures

Preface

Trying to summarize the essentials of macroeconomic theory in 2011 is no easy task. The financial crisis has shaken not only Western economies but also the macroeconomic profession, and the field has recently been the object of strong criticism. In particular, the notion that markets are self-correcting and always in equilibrium, as emphasized by the dominant dynamic general equilibrium (DGE) tradition, appears to have taken a heavy blow. However, the jury is still out on the areas that should be considered as failures and the areas that constitute the future of research.

The overall aim of this text is to provide a compact overview of what are currently regarded as the most important theoretical contributions to macroeconomic analysis. It is intended to present the core of advanced macroeconomic theory, the essential knowledge that all master's degree students in macroeconomics should be equipped with. As alluded to above, any such compilation of relevant knowledge inevitably has to make difficult judgments on what should be included and what should not. Views on the proper priority of relevant macroeconomic theory will very much depend on the orientation of the individual scholar and it is quite likely that such priority lists vary widely among macro teachers in the profession. Although I choose to include some theoretical contributions that are not usually included in macro textbooks and exclude others, I would certainly not claim that my choices are necessarily the most "appropriate" ones. Rather, they reflect to a large degree my own orientation and interests.

In this book, I have made the following basic priorities. Compared with many existing texts, I have emphasized the long run rather than the short run. The reason is partly that an increasing share of the most recent research in the leading journals is focused on long-run issues and partly that it appears to me that the theory of short-run (business cycle) fluctuations in the economy is not in good shape at the moment. Unlike any other macro textbook that I know of, this text includes a presentation of the Malthusian growth model. In order to understand the pattern of macro developments in countries like India and China and the historical pattern in Europe, it seems essential to include a discussion about the interaction between population and economic growth in economic development as discussed by Malthusian theory.

Sections on long-run growth are included mainly at the expense of short-run analysis such as business cycle theory. This text includes one chapter on the key features of DGE modeling, but I do not delve deeply into this type of framework. A more extensive section is devoted to a model of financial crises and bank runs. In the chapters on monetary and fiscal policy, I have further chosen to focus on models emphasizing political economy and institutional features. The political economy of market failures and imperfect institutions is currently a very active research agenda in economics and this text taps into some of that recent literature. In the chapter on consumption, I have further tried to include some of the most recent insights gained from research in behavioral economics.

Unlike the standard advanced textbooks in microeconomics, the models that are surveyed below do not emerge from a core set of assumptions that are then extended and applied in different directions, neither is the analysis based on a small number of key equations as in certain macro textbooks. Despite recent efforts, macroeconomic theory is still not a coherent body of theory in the same way as microeconomics or econometrics is. The DGE program was clearly an attempt to provide such a coherent framework, but recent events have put that effort into a less favorable light.[1]

The "workhorse" model for most chapters is, however, the well-known two-period, representative agent model of consumer optimization with a utility function given by $U = u(c_1) + \beta u(c_2)$ that is maximized subject to varying constraints. The majority of all models presented are thus "micro-founded", which should make the links to microeconomic theory more easily recognizable. Several of the chapters start off with a typical Keynesian model, which is then contrasted to models founded in individual household behavior and characterized by rational expectations and intertemporal optimization.

A key motivation of this text in comparison with the literature in the field is its condensed form. As a rule, most advanced textbooks in macroeconomics are about 500–600 pages long, mixing theory with somewhat randomly chosen empirical applications. This text is intended to be less than half as long as a standard textbook and to serve more or less as a reference source on modern macro theory. It is my hope that it will direct impatient readers (like myself) quickly to the main results. Admittedly, this writing approach might run the risk of alienating readers who rely more on texts focusing on the intuition behind models. Such readers might want to gather deeper intuitive insights from other sources, for instance from articles or more comprehensive macroeconomic textbooks.

A further and important delimitation of this work is that it will *not* discuss empirical tests of the theories surveyed. The reason is partly that I want to keep the text compact, but also that it is my impression that researchers seem to be somewhat more in agreement about what they think are the most relevant models, as compared with what they consider to be the most successful empirical tests of those models. Theory also changes more slowly than the stock of empirical results. This text should ideally be complemented with selected readings on empirical motivations and applications of the theories presented.

The book is intended to be suitable for a master's course in macro theory, lasting for about half a semester. Certain sections or chapters might also serve as an introduction to macroeconomics for nonspecialized graduate students. Readers are presumed to be relatively well equipped with calculus and algebra. A fairly strong background knowledge of both micro and macro theory is taken for granted.

The text has emerged from my experience of teaching advanced macro theory at the University of Gothenburg. Special thanks are due to my former teacher and most ardent reviewer Wlodek Bursztyn for having provided extensive comments on several previous versions (we still do not agree on certain aspects . . .). I have also benefited from many valuable discussions with Heather Congdon Fors and Per Krusell regarding macro theory in general. Oded Galor, Halvor Mehlum, Bo Sandelin, Joachim Smend, Olof Johansson-Stenman, David Weil, and three anonymous referees have commented on certain sections and provided valuable input. I am also indebted to several students who have commented on parts of the manuscript and pointed out errors. The mathematical appendix is a modified variant of a section prepared by Elias Tsakas. Lastly, I have very much appreciated my ongoing discussions with Rob Langham at Routledge, who encouraged me to write this book. All comments and suggestions for improvements are much appreciated.

Ola Olsson
(ola.olsson@economics.gu.se)
Floda, Sweden
May 2011

1 Introduction

1.1 The issues

Macroeconomics is the study of the aggregate economy of a country. It seeks to understand how the economic decisions of individual persons and firms are translated through markets into aggregate economic outcomes. Variables of interest in macroeconomic analysis are, for instance, the level and change of gross domestic product, the aggregate level of investment, government debt, inflation, and unemployment.

The macro economy affects individuals both directly and indirectly. More or less all individuals in modern economies are, for instance, subject to income taxation, are affected by bank interest rates, receive some kind of government subsidy, and control household budgets whose real value depends on the aggregate price level.

Macroeconomics is distinguished from microeconomics primarily in the sense that the ultimate dependent variables are different. Microeconomics studies the behavior of individuals or firms in order to understand individual choices. Macroeconomics also increasingly starts off with the modeling of a "representative" individual or firm that maximizes utility or profits, but the dependent variable is aggregate outcomes on a national level.

Macroeconomic outcomes are central to politics within countries. Questions like those below are discussed at more or less every general election (as well as in between elections) in the Western world:

- What policies are most effective against unemployment, and how should the government or the central bank fight inflation?
- How can economic growth be increased?
- How should governments stabilize short-run fluctuations and business cycles?
- What is a sustainable level of government debt?

In an international economy with interwoven markets, macroeconomics is also a central theme in international politics. A recurrent issue in international economic policy-making has been the determination of exchange rates between currencies. Another topic which has an important impact on international relations is current account levels and deficits or surpluses in the balance of trade. In summary, macroeconomics is a central field for anyone with an interest in economic policy or economic development.

1.2 The national accounts identity

The main building block of macroeconomic theory is the national accounts identity, which shows the gross domestic product (GDP) of a country. Total GDP, denoted by Y_t, measures the total value of all final goods and services that have been produced in a country during one year.[1] GDP is an example of a *flow* variable, one that is measured per unit of time. The other major type of variables are *stock* variables, such as the level of the capital stock or of accumulated public debt, which measure the level at a given point in time. We will return to this latter type of variables later.

Total GDP can be calculated in three ways, which all should yield the same result. The most common characterization of GDP is to study it from the *user side*, i.e. what total GDP is spent on. This is the *expenditure approach* to measuring total GDP and can be described by the equation

$$Y_t = C_t + I_t + G_t + X_t - M_t \tag{1.1}$$

In this key equation of macroeconomics, Y_t is total GDP as before at time t, C_t is aggregate private consumption, I_t is aggregate investment, G_t is government spending on goods and services, X_t is total exports from the country, and M_t is total imports. All these variables are flow variables.

Let us briefly take a closer look at these components of GDP. Aggregate private consumption C_t is typically the biggest item on the expenditure side and usually amounts to about half of total GDP. It includes personal spending on durable and nondurable goods and services during a year.[2] I_t is more specifically "gross domestic private investment" during one year. Investment is the acquisition of durable goods (with an expected life of more than one year) to be used as factors of production in the future, typically including machines and factories. Aggregate investment can in turn be split up into nonresidential investment, residential investment, and change in business inventories.

Government spending on goods and services G_t includes both government consumption (such as on salaries for teachers and judges) and investment (for instance, in government buildings). It also includes spending at all levels of government: state, regional, and local. Exports X_t is the value of goods and services produced within the country that are sold to people in foreign countries. Likewise, total imports M_t shows the value of goods and services produced outside the country that are bought by people inside the country.

This expenditure accounting of total GDP must be matched by the total income that all factors of production in the country earn during a given year. The *income side* of GDP is therefore

$$Y_t = \text{wages} + \text{rental incomes} + \text{profits} + \text{interest} \ldots \tag{1.2}$$

These incomes are eventually controlled by households in one way or another and are used for the expenditures above.

Furthermore, the total value of expenditures and incomes must be matched by the value added of aggregate production during a year. This is shown in the *production side* of the national accounts:

$$Y_t = \text{agriculture} + \cdots + \text{manufacturing} + \cdots$$
$$+ \text{professional and business services} \ldots \tag{1.3}$$

where the total values of production from all sectors of society are added.

The equation for the user side of GDP in (1.1) is the backbone of macro-economic theory from which the subsequent analysis is derived and extended in numerous ways. It also serves as a introduction to an outline of the exposition below.

1.3 Outline

The following chapters are organized as follows. We start off by analyzing the long-run determinants of total GDP, i.e. growth theory. Chapter 2 is devoted to the Malthusian model of growth, Chapter 3 presents the neoclassical (or Solow) growth model and its extensions, and Chapter 4 deals with endogenous growth models where technological progress plays a prominent role. In Chapter 5, we develop the overlapping generations model, which is long-run in nature and which is used also in the chapters ahead.

After the long run, we take a look at macroeconomic theory in the short and medium run. In Chapter 6, we study models on the behavior of total GDP and its components over the business cycle, i.e. a period of roughly five years. Chapter 7 discusses a recurrent phenomenon in capitalist economies: financial crises and bank runs. We then move on to analyze specifically the constituent parts of the expenditure side: consumption (and saving) in Chapter 8, investment and asset markets in Chapter 9, and one of the key markets for understanding the macro economy, the labor market, in Chapter 10.

In the third main section of the book, we analyze a broad range of topics related to macroeconomic policy. We begin by presenting the traditional IS–MP, aggregate supply and aggregate demand frameworks and the refinements suggested by the rational expectations view and the new Keynesian view in Chapter 11. We then go on to public finance and fiscal policy (Chapter 12), and inflation and monetary policy (Chapter 13). Lastly, we discuss international aspects of economic policy in Chapter 14.

Some basic mathematical results that are used throughout the text are provided in an appendix.

Part I

The Long Run

2 The Malthusian World

2.1 Introduction

In this chapter, we will describe a model of long-run economic growth that was applicable to all countries in the world up until the industrial revolution and which still is a highly relevant model for some developing countries. In this "Malthusian world" there is a strong link between income per capita and population growth, so that anything that increases aggregate income in a society will soon be neutralized by an increase in the size of the population. Hence, even despite periods of rapid technological progress, income per capita will remain at a fairly constant level. Recent empirical work on historical data has shown that standards of living indeed appear to have been roughly similar in Assyria around 1500 BC, in Egypt during Roman times, and in late eighteenth-century England (Clark 2007). This section is motivated by this stylized fact from economic history.

The main insights behind this model were proposed by Thomas Malthus (1798) but also critically hinge on the principle of diminishing returns to factors of production, and on theory that was further developed by David Ricardo. In the sections below, we will briefly discuss the theory of diminishing returns, the Malthusian model of long-run stagnation, and reasons for the eventual collapse of the Malthusian link. We will also show how fertility can be endogenously determined within a representative household.

2.2 The law of diminishing returns

One of the most fundamental building blocks of economics is the principle of diminishing returns. In production theory, diminishing returns means that if we produce a good, for instance shirts, by using two factors of production – say, workers and knitting machines – then if we keep the stock of machines fixed, each additional extra working hour will result in a smaller and smaller addition of new shirts on the margin. The reason is that workers need knitting machines to produce shirts and there will eventually be crowding effects if more and more workers have to share the same machines. This type of diminishing returns to labor or any other factor of production will be present in a single factory as well as in the economy as a whole, aggregated on a national level.

In order to illustrate this principle more rigorously, let us consider its mathematical properties. The fundamental assumption that all growth models share is that we can describe the total production in an economy (equivalent to total GDP) by an *aggregate production function*. In the pre-industrial era (and still in some of the poorest developing countries), the two most important factors of production were land and labor. Let us refer to the total number of workers in the economy as L and the total available land area as X. For simplicity, let us further imagine that the size of the labor force equals the size of the total population in a country. Land X is in fixed supply whereas population levels will change in response to changes in output, birth rates, and death rates, as will be shown below.

The aggregate production function for total output in the economy as a whole can be described as

$$Y = AX^{\alpha}L^{1-\alpha} \tag{2.1}$$

In this expression, Y is total output, A is a technology shift parameter, X is the fixed quantity of land, and L is the size of the population/labor force. The specific type of production function shown here is referred to as the *Cobb–Douglas functional form*. A might be thought of as capturing more broadly the general characteristics of the country in terms of, for instance, the state of technological knowledge or the quality of institutions. The parameter α ($0 < \alpha < 1$) is formally referred to as the *output elasticity of land*. Equivalently, $1 - \alpha$ is the *output elasticity of labor*. These elasticities show how total output Y responds to an increase in the production factor in question.

If we consider labor, its *marginal product* is defined as

$$\frac{\partial Y}{\partial L} = (1-\alpha)AX^{\alpha}L^{-\alpha} = (1-\alpha)A\left(\frac{X}{L}\right)^{\alpha} > 0 \tag{2.2}$$

The marginal product is always positive, indicating that if we increase the labor force in the country by one person, that person will always produce some extra output. However, as we see from (2.2), the marginal product will fall as we increase the number of workers since L now appears in the denominator. Formally, we can also show this by taking the second derivative:

$$\frac{\partial^2 Y}{\partial L^2} = -\alpha(1-\alpha)AX^{\alpha}L^{-\alpha-1} < 0$$

Thus, the Cobb–Douglas functional form ensures that Y has a *concave* relationship with L.

Note also that we can express total output per worker or per capita y as

$$\frac{Y}{L} = y = \frac{AX^{\alpha}L^{1-\alpha}}{L} = A\left(\frac{X}{L}\right)^{\alpha} = Ax^{\alpha} \tag{2.3}$$

where x is land per capita. Output per capita is one of the most often used indicators of standards of living in a country and is highly correlated with factors such as life expectancy, levels of education, the rule of law, and political freedom. We will refer to it frequently in the pages ahead.

From the expression in (2.3), it is clear that output per capita will fall with a greater level of population in the Malthusian model. On the one hand, one more worker means a little bit more output, but it also means another person to share total production with. The latter negative effect dominates. The first and second derivatives show us that

$$\frac{\partial y}{\partial L} = -\alpha A X^{\alpha} L^{-\alpha-1} < 0, \quad \frac{\partial^2 y}{\partial L^2} = \alpha(1+\alpha) A X^{\alpha} L^{-\alpha-2} > 0$$

which confirms what we just said.

2.3 The Malthusian trap

The key feature of the Malthusian model is that output per capita is strongly linked to population growth. In order to illustrate this, let us consider a very simple setup where the level of population at current time t is equal to last year's population level L_{t-1}, plus the number of births during year t, B_t, minus the number of deaths during the same year, D_t:

$$L_t = L_{t-1} + B_t(y_{t-1}) - D_t(y_{t-1}) \tag{2.4}$$

The central feature is that both B_t and D_t are functions of output per capita lagged one year, y_{t-1}. Birth rates increase with y_{t-1} such that $B'_t(y_{t-1}) > 0$ whereas $D'_t(y_{t-1}) < 0$. With an increase in output per capita, the supply of food increases, which allows families to grow. Likewise, the higher food consumption associated with a larger output at a given size of the population means that people die to a lesser extent from disease.[1]

The relationships between births, deaths, and the sizes of population and output per capita are drawn in Figure 2.1. In the figure, we assume for simplicity that B_t and D_t are linear functions of y. In the lower graph, we have drawn the negative convex relationship between y and L as stipulated by (2.3). The main insight from the figure is that output per capita will tend to converge towards an equilibrium level given by y^*. In the Malthusian model, y^* is often referred to as the *subsistence level* since it is inevitably at a quite low level that is not far above the level of income that allows people to survive. At this level, population ceases to grow and $L_t - L_{t-1} = B_t(y^*) - D_t(y^*) = 0$.

To see that y^* is an equilibrium, consider a relatively high level of initial output y^0. At this level of affluence, many children are born and relatively few people die of disease. Hence population levels increase, which pushes y to the left in the figure. The economy comes to rest again at y^* where output per capita has fallen to its subsistence level.

An even more grim situation is of course if the economy instead starts off to the left of y^*. In this situation, people are starving, few children are born, and many

Birth rates, death rates

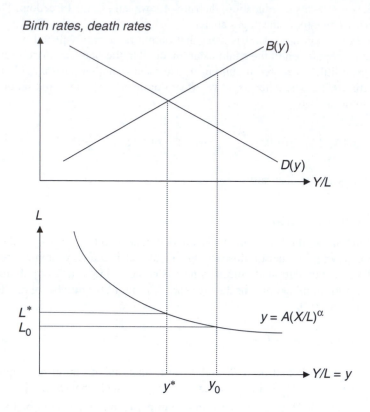

Figure 2.1 The Malthusian trap.

people die from disease. The level of the population shrinks, which gradually causes output per capita to rise. Back at y^*, normal times resume.

Consider now a positive technological shock such as the use of the plow or the introduction of windmills in the Middle Ages. Such a shock will appear as an increase in A in (2.3) and as an outward shift of the y-curve in the lower panel of Figure 2.2. This will temporarily cause output per capita to rise to $y' > y^*$. However, this new situation of prosperity will soon lead to a higher birth rate and a lower death rate, which will cause the population to grow. When population has grown to $L^{*,\text{new}} > L^*$, income per capita is back at its old level y^*. The only lasting result of a positive technology shock during the Malthusian era is thus a larger population.

As was mentioned above, several developing economies in the world that are dominated by subsistence agriculture are still caught in the Malthusian trap. Consider an extended drought of several years, such as happened in the African Sahel in 1985. In terms of Figure 2.2, such a shift would be like a negative shock to A_t and would cause the y-curve in the lower bar to shift leftwards so that income fell

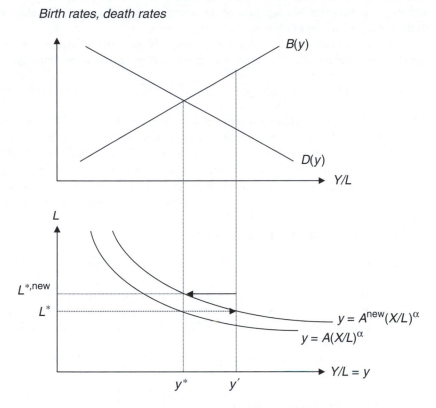

Figure 2.2 Technological progress in the Malthusian model.

below its subsistence level. If such populations are left to themselves, famine will set in and people will start dying of starvation. Starvation would, however, cause income levels per capita to start rising again, according to the Malthusian logic. Eventually, the economy would return to the old equilibrium level but this time with a much smaller population.

In the modern era, most Western governments would find such mass starvations unacceptable and provide emergency aid in the form of food and other relief. Such an intervention is of course highly commendable from a moral point of view, but it does not remove the Malthusian trap from the affected economy. If a downward adjustment of population levels does not take place, the country will be caught with a too large population that the country itself cannot feed. In this way, many of the poorest countries become dependent on aid.

2.4   Endogenous fertility

In the model above, we simply assumed that the number of births B_t was positively associated with the level of income y_{t-1} during the Malthusian era. Ashraf and

Galor (2010) demonstrate how this association can be derived explicitly from a model of a utility-maximizing household that can choose between having children and enjoying a high level of individual consumption.

Let us assume that total output in the economy is the same as in (2.1) and that the (Cobb–Douglas) utility function of a representative individual at time t is

$$U_t = c_t^{1-\beta} n_t^{\beta} \tag{2.5}$$

where $c_t = C_t/L_t$ is consumption per capita in the economy, $n_t \geq 0$ is the number of surviving children that the individual gives birth to, and $\beta \in (0, 1)$ is a parameter reflecting the relative importance of children for the individual's utility. The function makes two simplifying assumptions. First, we imagine that this single (hermaphrodite) individual can choose how many children he or she wishes to have. Second, we imagine that children can come in nondiscrete amounts (i.e. we allow $n_t = 1.2$ to be a possibility).

The budget constraint for the individual is

$$c_t + \rho n_t = y_t \tag{2.6}$$

where $\rho > 0$ is the relative cost of raising children and y_t is income per capita as specified above. This constraint shows that the individual faces a trade-off between own consumption c_t and having children. If the person decides to have children, the cost per child is fixed at ρ.

The utility function and the budget constraint together define a utility-maximization problem:

$$\max_{n_t} U_t \quad \text{subject to } c_t + \rho n_t = y_t$$

A straightforward way of solving this problem is simply to rewrite the budget constraint as $c_t = y_t - \rho n_t$ and then replace c_t with this expression in the utility function. If we further take logs of the utility function, the problem at hand reduces to

$$\max_{n_t} \ln U_t = (1 - \beta) \ln(y_t - \rho n_t) + \beta \ln n_t$$

The first-order condition for maximum is[2]

$$\frac{\partial \ln U_t}{\partial n_t} = -\frac{(1-\beta)\rho}{y_t - \rho n_t} + \frac{\beta}{n_t} = 0$$

By rearranging this condition, we obtain

$$\beta(y_t - \rho n_t) = (1 - \beta)\rho n \Longrightarrow (1 - \beta)\rho n_t + \beta \rho n_t = \rho n_t = \beta y_t$$

$$\Longrightarrow n_t^* = \frac{\beta y_t}{\rho}$$

Thus, the utility-maximizing (optimal) fertility level n_t^* is a linear function of the income level per capita y_t. This result is a close analogy to the assumption above of a function $B_t(y_{t-1})$. The number of children decreases with the cost of having children ρ. Note that $n_t^* > 1$ implies that the population is growing.

If we insert the derived level of n_t^* back into the budget constraint, we can solve for c_t^*:

$$c_t^* + \rho n_t^* = y_t = c_t^* + \beta y_t \Longrightarrow c_t^* = (1 - \beta) y_t$$

The growth of the total level of population between periods t and $t + 1$ is given by

$$L_{t+1} = n_t^* L_t = \frac{\beta y_t L_t}{\rho} = \frac{\beta A L_t^{1-\alpha} X^\alpha}{\rho} = \varphi(A, L_t) \tag{2.7}$$

where we have substituted $y_t = A(X/L_t)^\alpha$ from (2.3). The expression in (2.7) implies that L_{t+1} is a positive and concave function φ of L_t and a linear function of the level of technology A_t.[3] The concavity of L_{t+1} in L_t arises since the first derivative is $\varphi_L > 0$ whereas the second is $\varphi_{LL} < 0$. In Figure 2.3, we have drawn (2.7) in (L_{t+1}, L_t) space.

The figure includes the function $\varphi(A, L_t)$ as well as a 45° line where $L_{t+1} = L_t$. The crossing happens at $L_t = L_{t+1} = L^*$. This is the equilibrium population size in the model. To see why, consider for a moment a situation to the left of L^* where $L_t < L^*$. At this level, $n_t^* > 1$ and the population grows. Analogously, to the right of L^*, $n_t^* < 1$ and the population shrinks. Only at $L_t = L_{t+1} = L^*$ will the economy come to "rest" in equilibrium.

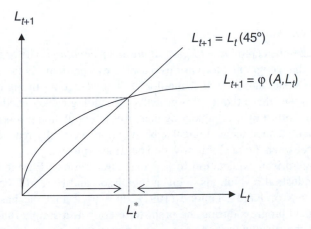

Figure 2.3 Equilibrium population size.

If we insert L^* into (2.7), we can solve for the equilibrium level of population density:

$$\frac{L^*}{X} = \frac{1}{x^*} = \left(\frac{\beta A}{\rho}\right)^{\frac{1}{\alpha}}$$

The real-world equivalent of this expression could, for instance, be population per square kilometer. Equilibrium population density during the Malthusian era should thus increase with a country's total productivity or level of technological sophistication, just like above. Ashraf and Galor (2010) find strong support for this hypothesis in their empirical study.

2.5   The collapse of the Malthusian link

By 1800, the United Kingdom was the first country in the world to break free of the Malthusian trap during the industrial revolution. The United Kingdom was soon followed by other Western countries, and later by yet more countries in other parts of the world in a process that is still going on. This *modern growth regime* was characterized by the following empirically observable features: (1) a fall in birth rates B and an end to the link with income per capita y (death rates D continued to fall with y); (2) an overall increase in levels of education; (3) an increase in the growth of technological knowledge A; (4) as a direct consequence of (1)–(3), a dramatic increase in output per capita far beyond subsistence levels.

Although most economic historians agree on these stylized facts, their models of how this change came about and why it was initiated in western Europe after 1800 rather than in, say, thirteenth-century India, differ to some extent. Here we will only focus on some of the most prominent explanations.

2.5.1   Geography and institutions

One tradition emphasizes the central role of *geography* and *technology*. The basic idea in these works is that geography, for various reasons, was particularly favorable in Europe for the steady advance of technological knowledge A. In highly simplified terms, it is argued that although this growth of technological knowledge in Europe was generally offset by accompanying increases in population levels in the standard Malthusian manner, technological sophistication eventually reached a critical threshold level when the rate of innovation became explosive.

One such technology-driven explanation for the early transition of Europe to the agricultural and industrial revolutions is given by Olsson and Hibbs (2005). In the spirit of the work of Jared Diamond (1997), they argue that the basic process for technological progress during the prehistoric era was a simple function of the quality of the surrounding environment. In particular, technological progress was faster in environments that were rich in potentially useful factors of production, i.e. of suitable species for plant and animal domestication. As convincingly shown by Diamond (1997), Western Eurasia (Europe and the Middle East) was uniquely endowed with such species, which in turn explained the early transition to sedentary agriculture, civilization and the rise of states.[4]

Olsson and Hibbs model the growth of technological knowledge during prehistoric times as

$$A_{t+1} - A_t = A_t \gamma E_i$$

where $\gamma > 0$ is a parameter invariant across regions and E_i is the "wealth" of the environment in region i in terms of useful plants and animals for domestication. Regions that were generously endowed thus had fast growth and eventually reached a critical level $\bar{A}$ where the transition to Neolithic agriculture happened early.[5] The transition to agriculture then implied that a certain part of the population was freed from producing and formed a new elite of specialists that would be essential for the subsequent rapid advance of science and technology. The Neolithic revolution thus created the first instance of endogenous technological growth, i.e. the purposeful creation of new knowledge through the allocation of labor resources to a new sector.

In Olsson and Hibbs (2005), the growth rate of technology changed shape to become

$$\frac{A_{t+1} - A_t}{A_t} = g(a_t L_t)$$

where $a_t < 1$ is the share of the total labor force L_t at time t engaged in endogenous knowledge creation, and $g(a_t L_t)$ is a function of $a_t L_t$ such that $g'(a_t L_t) > 0$. In Diamond's (1997) informal account and in Olsson and Hibbs' model, the very early creation of this knowledge-producing sector is the key to understanding why Western Eurasia could start to dominate other continents from AD 1500 despite the fact that Europe was not richer in per capita terms than any other part of the world. According to this view, the industrial revolution was just a natural extension to a development that had its roots in the transition to agriculture.

This theory has been criticized by a direction of research emphasizing the central role of *economic and political institutions*, i.e. the fundamental rules that societies live by. Acemoglu et al (2005) demonstrate that Western colonialism played an important role in the accumulation of capital in western coastal Europe. The inflow of capital strengthened the political power of a merchant class in countries like Britain and the Netherlands, which in turn led to reforms and stronger institutional constraints against the executive *vis-à-vis* the citizens. In Spain, however, the inflow of capital only led to the enrichment of an elite around the Crown and fostered rent-seeking behavior rather than production and investment. The institutional changes in Britain and the Netherlands eventually triggered the industrial revolution.

2.5.2   *Galor and Weil's unified growth model*

The models above are not concerned with the more exact mechanism whereby the link between population growth and income per capita is broken. Galor and Weil (2000), however, focus explicitly on the dynamics of this process. One of the main assumptions in their model is that parents face a basic trade-off between *child quantity* (number of children) and *child quality* (children's level of education).[6] In this section we present an extremely simplified version of Galor and Weil's model.

Parents divide their time between work and childrearing. Time spent on one child in period t is in turn divided between basic childrearing τ and education so that the child's level of education in the next period is e_{t+1}. Let the family's total number of children in period t be denoted by n_t and let the total time available to parents be normalized to unity. Hence, the time budget constraint for parents is

$$n_t(\tau + e_{t+1}) \leq 1$$

The time budget constraint shows that parents face a trade-off between having many children (a high n_t) and giving them a good level of future education e_{t+1}. This is similar to what Becker and Lewis (1973) refer to as the child quantity/child quality trade-off. If, for instance, $n_t(\tau + e_{t+1}) = 1$ applies, then in order to increase e_{t+1} we must necessarily decrease n_t in a proportional manner.[7] In the full version of the model, Galor and Weil (2000) derive the optimal allocation of time spent on the two activities and show that it will to a great extent depend on the parents' preference structure. It is well known, however, that during most of human history, the trade-off was such that $e_{t+1} = 0$. A central element of the breaking of the Malthusian trap was precisely that levels of education started rising and the number of children born in each family started falling.

So why did families start to substitute child quantity for child quality? In the model, Galor and Weil derive the result that the optimal level of e_{t+1} is a function of the growth rate of technological knowledge such that $e_t = e(g_t)$. The logic is simply that the greater the advancement of technological knowledge in a society, the higher will the optimal level of education be. The derivatives are $\partial e_t/\partial g_t = e_g \geq 0$ and $\partial^2 e_t/\partial g_t^2 = e_{gg} \leq 0$.

Let us also assume that the growth rate of technological knowledge is given by

$$\frac{A_{t+1} - A_t}{A_t} = g_{t+1} = g(e_t, L_t)$$

In this expression, the growth rate g is a positive function of e_t and L_t. A higher level of education in the population e_t is associated with faster technological progress, and, likewise, a larger population means more potential innovators. In formal terms, the partial derivatives are assumed to be $\partial g/\partial e_t = g_e > 0$, $\partial g/\partial L_t = g_L > 0$, and $\partial^2 g/\partial e_t^2 = g_{ee} < 0$. Once parents start investing in education for their children, there might thus be a kind of positive feedback loop between education and technological progress.

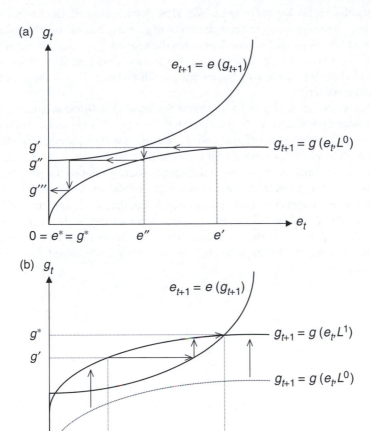

Figure 2.4 (a) A Malthusian trap in the evolution of technology and education in the Galor–Weil model. (b) Escape from the Malthusian trap in the Galor–Weil model due to an increase in population ($L^1 > L^0$).

The basic relationship between the two variables is shown in Figures 2.4a and 2.4b. In these figures, we have drawn both the $e_{t+1} = e(g_{t+1})$ and the $g_{t+1} = g(e_t, L_t)$ curves simultaneously. Their slopes are as derived above.[8] Note that below a certain level of technological progress g_t, the optimal level of education e_t is zero.

Now consider an economy that starts off at a level of education $e' > 0$. At this level, next year's technological progress is fairly high at $g' > 0$. The level of population is $L^0 > 0$. However, at this level of g, education in the next period is discouraged and will fall to $e'' < e'$, as indicated by the arrow. At this lower level of education, technological progress will slow down and g will fall further to $g'' < g'$. Hence, in the economy at hand, there is a negative feedback loop between education and technology that eventually causes the economy to reach an equilibrium where $e^* = g^* = 0$. Since no time is spent on education, parents will spend all their nonworking time on having babies and n_t will be large. This is the typical Malthusian trap scenario.

Consider now another economy (or the same economy at a different date) as in Figure 2.4b where population is $L^1 > L^0$ so that the $g(e_t, L^0)$ curve has shifted upward to $g(e_t, L^0)$. If we start off at e' and g', education will be strongly encouraged by the high level of g, so that e will increase in the next period. The higher level of education in turn spurs faster technological progress, and so the economy enters a positive virtuous circle that settles down at equilibrium levels $e^*, g^* > 0$. Since parents' time budget constraint has not expanded, they will substitute child quantity n_t for child quality e_t. As total production in society starts rising fast due to technological progress, the combined effect of a lower n_t and a higher g_t makes income per capita rise explosively. The economy has escaped from the Malthusian trap.

3 The Solow Growth Model

3.1 Introduction

In this third chapter, we will analyze the determinants of wealth and poverty during the industrial era among nations most of which have managed to escape from the Malthusian trap. Rather than focusing on short-term phenomena like business cycles, we will try to understand long-run patterns of development, for example why some of the richest countries such as Switzerland and Norway have a level of GDP that is about one hundred times greater than the GDP of some of the poorest countries such as Niger and Haiti.[1]

Population growth will play no important role in this framework since it is assumed to have stabilized at relatively low (exogenous) levels. The key factor of production is instead physical capital and the key process is that of *convergence*, showing how economies that initially start off with relatively low levels of physical capital per worker should grow faster than relatively richer countries.

The neoclassical growth model builds fundamentally on the work of Robert Solow (1956) and has become one of the most important models in macroeconomic research. We start by deriving the well-known $\dot{k}$-equation and the most important implications that follow from it such as convergence. In the final sections, we present some extensions to the Solow model where we demonstrate how technological progress and human capital can be included in the basic framework.

3.2 Basic assumptions

The main contribution of the Solow growth model from a theoretical point of view is that it makes the accumulation of physical capital endogenous, as will soon become clear.[2]

The simplest version of the Solow growth model assumes an aggregate production function F of the following form:

$$Y_t = F(K(t), L(t)) \tag{3.1}$$

where Y_t is total GDP measured from the production side, $K(t)$ is total physical capital that is a function of time t, and $L(t)$ is the aggregate labor force.[3] $K(t)$

might be thought of as the total stock of factories and machines in a country and $L(t)$ as the total number of workers. K and L (we will henceforth usually drop the time (t) notation for ease of exposition) are thus production factors or inputs in the aggregate production process.

We also make the following more technical assumptions:

- *Constant returns to scale*: $F(\lambda K, \lambda(L)) = \lambda F(K, L)$.
- *All factors of production have positive but diminishing marginal returns*: $\frac{\partial F}{\partial K} = F_K > 0, \frac{\partial^2 F}{\partial K^2} = F_{KK} < 0$ at all levels of K; $\frac{\partial F}{\partial L} = F_L > 0, \frac{\partial^2 F}{\partial L^2} < 0$ at all levels of L.

The constant-returns assumption means that if we, for instance, double the levels of K and L simultaneously, we will get a doubling of total output.[4] The second assumption implies that F has a concave relationship with both production factors and that the marginal product is always positive. This is the same "Ricardian" assumption of diminishing returns as was used in the Malthusian model.

It is further assumed that we can transform the aggregate production function in the following way:

$$\frac{F(K, L)}{L} = F\left(\frac{K}{L}, \frac{L}{L}\right) = F\left(\frac{K}{L}, 1\right) = f(k), \quad \text{where } k = \frac{K}{L} \tag{3.2}$$

This transformation is referred to as the *intensive form* of (3.1) and k is formally referred to as *capital per worker*. As we shall see, using this intensive-form expression simplifies the algebra significantly in the sections ahead.

The intensive form of the production function has the same basic properties as above:

- $f(0) = 0$; $f'(k) > 0$; $f''(k) < 0$ at all levels of $k > 0$.

The most often used functional form for the production function in growth theory is *Cobb–Douglas*:

$$Y = F(K, L) = K^\alpha L^{1-\alpha} \tag{3.3}$$

Dividing through by L gives us the intensive form, or output per worker y:

$$y = f(k) = \frac{K^\alpha L^{1-\alpha}}{L} = K^\alpha L^{-\alpha} = \left(\frac{K}{L}\right)^\alpha = k^\alpha \tag{3.4}$$

3.3 Dynamics

All variables in the model are functions of time, so the next step is to specify their dynamics or *laws of motion*. The growth of labor L is in this setting assumed to be exogenously given, i.e. not explained by the model:

$$\frac{\partial L(t)}{\partial t} = \dot{L}(t) = nL, \quad \text{where } n > 0, \quad \text{implying } \frac{\dot{L}}{L} = n$$

In this expression, n is the (percentage) growth rate of the labor force (or of population size). Although time derivatives indicate instantaneous changes in the stocks, we normally think of $\frac{\dot{L}}{L}$, for instance, as the growth rate during a year, as in the national accounts.[5] A typical level for n would thus be 0.01–0.05.

The key dynamic equation in the Solow model is that specifying the rate of change in the physical capital stock:

$$\dot{K} = sY - \delta K \tag{3.5}$$

In this expression, $s > 0$ is the fraction of total output Y that is being saved and $\delta > 0$ is the capital depreciation rate, i.e. the fraction of total physical capital that is worn down every year. (Typical and often observed levels are $s = 0.2$ and $\delta = 0.05$.) The same expression can be restated as $sY = \dot{K} + \delta K = I$, which tells us that total savings sY can be used for *net investment* $\dot{K}$ (leading to actual increases in the capital stock) and *replacement investments* δK (replacing the capital that has been worn down), and which together sum to total aggregate investment I.

The Solow growth model implicitly assumes a closed economy without trade and where there is no government. Hence, the user side of the economy contains only investment and consumption (compare with the fundamental equation (1.1) above). Therefore, we can write

$$Y = \dot{K} + \delta K + C = I + C$$

where C is the aggregate level of consumption.

We want to express $\dot{K}$ in intensive form, i.e. we want to find $\dot{k}$. Recall that $k(t) = K(t)/L(t)$. Hence, by using the chain and quotient rules of differentiation, we can write

$$\begin{aligned}
\frac{\partial k(t)}{\partial t} = \dot{k} &= \frac{\dot{K}}{L} - \frac{K}{L^2}\dot{L} \\
&= \frac{\dot{K}}{L} - k\frac{\dot{L}}{L} = \frac{sY(t) - \delta K(t)}{L} - nk \\
&= sf(k) - (\delta + n)k
\end{aligned} \tag{3.6}$$

The expression in the third line of (3.6) is the central equation of the Solow growth model.

3.4 Equilibrium

The $\dot{k}$-equation can also be drawn as in Figure 3.1. The vertical axis simply shows levels whereas the horizontal axis shows capital per unit of effective labor, k.

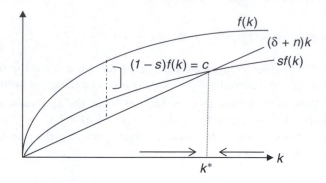

Figure 3.1 The neoclassical growth diagram.

The two most important lines here are the $sf(k)$ and $(\delta + n)k$ curves, where it is important to note that the former is concave since $f''(k) < 0$. $sf(k)$ is sometimes referred to as *the actual level* of investment and $(\delta + n)k$ as the *break-even level* of investment. Beyond these curves, however, there is also the $f(k)$ curve. Note that the vertical distance between the $sf(k)$ and $f(k)$ curves equals $c = C/L$, i.e. consumption per unit of labor.

At low levels of k, $\dot{k} > 0$, whereas at high levels of k, $\dot{k} < 0$. The only stable equilibrium in Figure 3.1 occurs at k^*, which is defined by the point where the $sf(k)$ and $(\delta + n)k$ curves cross. This is also the level of k where $\dot{k} = 0$, implying that K and L grow at a "balanced" rate.[6] k^* is often also referred to as the *steady-state equilibrium*.

3.5   Implications

3.5.1   Cobb–Douglas functional form

If we assume a Cobb–Douglas functional form for the production function as in (3.4), we will have the following $\dot{k}$-equation:

$$\dot{k} = sk^\alpha - (\delta + n)k$$

From this expression, we can also derive the growth rate per worker (by using the chain rule):

$$\frac{\dot{y}}{y} = \frac{\frac{\partial(k^\alpha)}{\partial t}}{k^\alpha} = \frac{\alpha k^{\alpha-1}\dot{k}}{k^\alpha} = \frac{\alpha\dot{k}}{k} \tag{3.7}$$

$$= s\alpha k^{\alpha-1} - \alpha(\delta + n) = \frac{s\alpha}{k^{1-\alpha}} - \alpha(\delta + n)$$

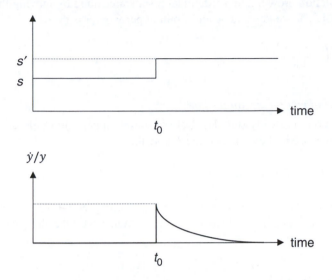

Figure 3.2 Impact on growth rate per worker of an increase in the savings rate.

In the short run, the growth rate will depend on the initial level of k since economies with a low level of k will have $\dot{k} > 0$ and will grow faster. However, as k increases, the economy will gradually approach its steady-state level k^* where $\dot{k} = 0$. Furthermore, an increase in the savings rate s that happens in a steady state will temporarily increase the growth rate since it will turn $\dot{k}$ positive. The long-run effect, however, should be zero when k has moved to a new (and higher) equilibrium level (see Figure 3.2). Similarly, a sudden increase in population growth will lead to a period of negative growth, until the economy settles at a lower equilibrium level of k and an associated lower level of output per worker. This prediction of temporary effects on the growth rate but permanent effects on the steady-state levels of output is among the most central predictions from the model and has been tested numerous times in the empirical literature.

We can also solve for the steady-state level of k:

$$\dot{k} = 0 \Longrightarrow s(k^*)^{\alpha} = (\delta + n)k^* \tag{3.8}$$

$$\Longrightarrow (k^*)^{\alpha - 1} = \frac{(\delta + n)}{s} \Longrightarrow k^* = \left(\frac{\delta + n}{s}\right)^{\frac{1}{\alpha - 1}}$$

$$= k^* = \left(\frac{s}{\delta + n}\right)^{\frac{1}{1 - \alpha}}$$

Note that we want to carry out the last step in order to have the exponent positive ($\frac{1}{\alpha - 1} < 0$). This expression for the steady-state level clearly shows that k^* will increase with the savings rate s, and decrease with the capital depreciation rate δ

and with the population growth rate n. Identical results are found by moving the curves in Figure 3.1. The steady-state level of output per worker is thus

$$y^* = (k^*)^\alpha = \left(\frac{s}{\delta + n}\right)^{\frac{\alpha}{1-\alpha}}$$

3.5.2 Golden rule of capital accumulation

What is the impact on the steady-state level of consumption per unit of effective labor c^* from an increase in the savings rate s? Note that

$$c^* = (1 - s)f(k^*) = f(k^*) - (n + \delta)k^* \tag{3.9}$$

We know from (3.8) that k^* increases with s, but in the expression (3.9) there is both a positive and a negative effect of k^* on c^*. When we take the partial derivative, we get

$$\frac{\partial c^*}{\partial s} = [f'(k^*) - (n + \delta)]\frac{\partial k^*}{\partial s}$$

The sign of this expression will be determined by the sign of the term in square brackets (know that $\frac{\partial k^*}{\partial s} > 0$ always holds). Since $f'(k^*)$ is very large at small levels of k (see Figure 3.1), we can infer that $\frac{\partial c^*}{\partial s} > 0$ when k is small, whereas at greater levels of k it will be the case that $\frac{\partial c^*}{\partial s} < 0$. Hence, there is a level of k^*, referred to as $k^{*,\text{gold}}$, when $\frac{\partial c^*}{\partial s} = 0$:

$$\frac{\partial c^*}{\partial s} = 0 \quad \text{when } f'(k^{*,\text{gold}}) = n + \delta \tag{3.10}$$

Beyond this level of k, a further capital accumulation will decrease intensive consumption c. The level $k^{*,\text{gold}}$ is referred to as s^{gold}. The intuition about this *golden rule of capital accumulation* is that it is only useful to increase the savings rate up to a certain level.

3.5.3 Convergence

The model above has some strong predictions about *convergence*, i.e. that countries that start off with a lower level of k should experience a higher growth rate of output per worker. Another way of illustrating the convergence property is described below.[7]

If we insert a Cobb–Douglas production function $f(k) = k^\alpha$ into the model above, it was shown that we can write the growth rate of output per worker as:

$$\frac{\dot{y}}{y} = \alpha(sk^{\alpha-1} - \delta - n)$$

Since $\frac{Y}{L} = k^\alpha = y$, we can express k as $k = y^{\frac{1}{\alpha}}$. Inserting into the growth equation above yields

$$\frac{\dot{y}}{y} = \alpha(sy^{\frac{\alpha-1}{\alpha}} - \delta - n) = \alpha\left(\frac{s}{y^{\frac{1-\alpha}{\alpha}}} - \delta - n\right) \tag{3.11}$$

Variants of this expression form the basis of the cross-country empirical studies on the determinants of economic growth. The key prediction concerning convergence is that the growth rate of output per worker should decrease with its initial level, y. In other words, holding all other factors constant, poorer countries should grow faster than richer ones. A country's growth rate during the convergence process should further increase with its savings rate s, and decrease with the population growth rate n and with the capital depreciation rate δ. The growth rate of rich countries that have reached their steady state will depend on the exogenous parameter g.

The convergence result suggests that the poorest countries in the world should experience the highest growth rates. Although we know that many previously poor countries have experienced very fast growth rates in recent decades – for instance China, India, and Botswana – other countries have experienced stagnant growth or even growth collapses. Some countries, such as DR Congo and Zambia, have even seen their levels of income per capita fall by half. We will return to this issue below.

3.6 Extensions

The simple version of the Solow growth function presented above provides the basic intuition behind the important convergence property and the central role played by physical capital accumulation. It abstracts, however, from numerous factors that are believed to be central for economic growth to occur even in the medium run. Two of the most important of these factors are technological progress and human capital accumulation.

3.6.1 Technological progress

Technological progress can be readily included in the basic model above. As in Chapter 2, let us refer to the level of technological knowledge at time t as A_t. Most growth models further assume that technology is primarily *labor augmenting*, i.e. that A_t increases workers' level of productivity. We will refer to the composite production factor $A_t L_t$ as *effective labor*.[8] The aggregate production function then becomes

$$Y = F(K, AL) = K^\alpha (AL)^{1-\alpha}$$

Let us further assume that the growth rate of technology is exogenously given by

$$\frac{\dot{A}_t}{A_t} = g > 0$$

The intensive form is now written as $\kappa = K/AL$ and is referred to as *capital per unit of effective labor*. The time derivative of κ is

$$\dot{\kappa} = \frac{\dot{K}}{AL} - \frac{KL}{(AL)^2}\dot{A} - \frac{KA}{(AL)^2}\dot{L}$$

$$= \frac{sY - \delta K}{AL} - \kappa\frac{\dot{A}}{A} - \kappa\frac{\dot{L}}{L} = s\hat{f}(\kappa) - \kappa(\delta + g + n)$$

where $\hat{f}(\kappa) = F(K, AL)/AL$. As in the section above, the economy will be in a steady-state equilibrium when $\dot{\kappa} = 0$, which happens at a level $\kappa^* = \left(\frac{s}{\delta+g+n}\right)^{\frac{1}{1-\alpha}}$. The equilibrium level of capital per unit of effective labor thus decreases with the technological growth rate.

Since output per capita can now be expressed as $Y/L = K^\alpha(AL)^{1-\alpha}/L = A\kappa^\alpha$, its growth rate is given by

$$\frac{\dot{y}}{y} = \frac{\dot{A}}{A} + \alpha\frac{\dot{\kappa}}{\kappa} = g + \alpha\left(\frac{s\hat{f}(\kappa)}{\kappa} - \delta - g - n\right)$$

Note that when $\kappa = \kappa^*$, the term inside the parentheses will be equal to zero. The equilibrium growth rate of output per capita is then simply $g > 0$. Hence, rich countries at their equilibrium growth rates will only grow through technological progress. In the Solow model, this growth rate is exogenously given and we cannot say anything very interesting about it. The main aim of *endogenous growth theory*, which is the topic of the next chapter, is to derive this growth rate as the result of intentional human investments in research and development (R&D).

3.6.2   *Human capital*

The level of technological knowledge A_t is meant to capture the stock of production-relevant ideas that (in the absence of intellectual property rights) are free for anyone to use. In the economics terminology, we refer to ideas as *nonrival* goods that have the same basic character as most public goods. One idea can be used in thousands of places and situations at the same time.[9]

Human capital, on the other hand, is the skills and competencies embodied in people. The skills of a certain person cannot be used in two offices at the same time. Human capital is typically enhanced through education or learning and often depreciates with time due to obsolescence or because people tend to forget. In this sense, human capital has a lot in common with physical capital that also increases through investment and decreases through depreciation.

Mankiw et al (1992) extend the basic Solow model to also include human capital. In their model, the aggregate stock of human capital in an economy H is thought of as distinct from effective labor AL. They imagine an aggregate production function of the form

$$Y = F(K, H, AL) = K^\alpha H^\beta (AL)^{1-\alpha-\beta}$$

In their model, both physical capital and human capital grow endogenously. Let $\kappa = K/AL$, $\eta = H/AL$, and $\tilde{y} = K^\alpha H^\beta (AL)^{1-\alpha-\beta}/AL = \kappa^\alpha \eta^\beta$. The dynamics of the two stocks are given by

$$\dot{\kappa} = s_\kappa \kappa^\alpha \eta^\beta - \kappa(\delta + g + n)$$
$$\dot{\eta} = s_\eta \kappa^\alpha \eta^\beta - \eta(\delta + g + n)$$

The parameters $s_\kappa > 0$ and $s_\eta > 0$ reflect the share of total output per unit of effective labor $\tilde{y} = \kappa^\alpha \eta^\beta$ that is invested in physical capital and human capital, respectively. A share $1 - s_\kappa - s_\eta$ of total income is devoted to consumption. s_η might thus be seen as a country's rate of investment in education. As discussed in Chapter 2, this rate was very low in most countries until about 1800. For simplicity, it is assumed that both stocks have the same depreciation rate $\delta + g + n$.

The steady-state levels κ^* and η^* are found where $\dot{\kappa} = \dot{\eta} = 0$. Reaching the solution involves more algebra than before since we first have to solve for one of the two steady-state levels and then insert this solution into the expression for the other. In the first step, we find from $\dot{\kappa} = 0$ that

$$\kappa^* = \left(\frac{s_\kappa (\eta^*)^\beta}{\delta + g + n} \right)^{\frac{1}{1-\alpha}}$$

and from $\dot{\eta} = 0$ that

$$\eta^* = \left(\frac{s_\eta (\kappa^*)^\alpha}{\delta + g + n} \right)^{\frac{1}{1-\beta}}$$

If we then take logs of the two expressions above, we get

$$\ln \kappa^* = \frac{1}{1-\alpha} \ln \left(\frac{s_\kappa}{\delta + g + n} \right) + \frac{\beta}{1-\alpha} \ln \eta^* \tag{3.12}$$

$$\ln \eta^* = \frac{1}{1-\beta} \ln \left(\frac{s_\eta}{\delta + g + n} \right) + \frac{\alpha}{1-\beta} \ln \kappa^* \tag{3.13}$$

Inserting the expression for $\ln \eta^*$ in (3.13) into (3.12), we obtain

$$\ln \kappa^* = \frac{1}{1-\alpha} \ln \left(\frac{s_\kappa}{\delta + g + n} \right) + \frac{\beta}{(1-\alpha)(1-\beta)} \ln \left(\frac{s_\eta}{\delta + g + n} \right)$$
$$+ \frac{\alpha\beta}{(1-\alpha)(1-\beta)} \ln \kappa^*$$

Then manipulating the expression so that $\ln \kappa^*$ is isolated on the left-hand side,

$$\ln \kappa^* = \frac{1-\beta}{1-\alpha-\beta} \ln \left(\frac{s_\kappa}{\delta + g + n} \right) + \frac{\beta}{1-\alpha-\beta} \ln \left(\frac{s_\eta}{\delta + g + n} \right)$$

By taking the anti-log of this expression, we can express the closed-form solution as

$$\kappa^* = \left(\frac{s_\eta^\beta s_\kappa^{1-\beta}}{\delta + g + n} \right)^{\frac{1}{1-\alpha-\beta}}$$

By using the same methodology, we can also solve for η^*:

$$\eta^* = \left(\frac{s_\kappa^\alpha s_\eta^{1-\alpha}}{\delta + g + n} \right)^{\frac{1}{1-\alpha-\beta}}$$

A noteworthy feature of these expressions is that κ^* increases with s_η and that η^* increases with s_κ. This effect arises since a higher s_η increases the level of η and the level of available resources $\tilde{y}$, which means that there is a higher total income to be invested in physical capital.

The steady-state level of output per capita in this economy is

$$y^* = A_t(\kappa^*)^\alpha(\eta^*)^\beta = A_t \left(\frac{s_\eta^\beta s_\kappa^{1-\beta}}{\delta + g + n} \right)^{\frac{\alpha}{1-\alpha-\beta}} \left(\frac{s_\kappa^\alpha s_\eta^{1-\alpha}}{\delta + g + n} \right)^{\frac{\beta}{1-\alpha-\beta}}$$

$$= A_t \left(\frac{s_\eta^\alpha s_\kappa^\beta}{(\delta + g + n)^{\alpha+\beta}} \right)^{\frac{1}{1-\alpha-\beta}}$$

Since A_t is the only factor of production that does not converge to a steady-state level, the equilibrium growth rate of output per capita will be equal to g, as above.

4 Endogenous Growth Theory

4.1 Introduction

The Solow growth model has been criticized on two grounds: Firstly, the prediction that all countries should converge to the same long run growth rate does not appear to have materialized. Secondly, the engine of long-run growth, technological progress g, is left unexplained by the model.

In this chapter, we will take a closer look at endogenous growth theory, which attempts to explain how technological progress emerges as a consequence of more or less active choices by the agents in the economy. In particular, we will analyze how a separate R&D sector interacts with sectors producing intermediate and final goods. The presence of intellectual property rights means that intermediate goods-producing firms might in practice obtain a monopoly on the good they are producing. The later sections analyze the implications of incorporating assumptions of imperfect competition. The main contributors to this literature are Paul Romer (1986, 1990) and Aghion and Howitt (1992).

Due to the focus on technological progress, the current chapter is mainly relevant for relatively advanced developed economies where R&D plays a key role. Most countries in the world do not carry out any advanced R&D and only imitate the innovations carried out in Western countries. Section 4.6 contains a model where a social planner in a country can choose between imitation and innovation.

4.2 *AK* model

In a famous article, Romer (1986) argues that the tendency towards diminishing returns, which is a central feature of the Solow growth model, is perhaps exaggerated. According to Romer, it also appears as if certain types of policy have a more lasting impact on growth rates than in the Solow model. The simple solution to these aspects was offered by Rebelo's (1991) AK model.

Let us assume that the correct specification of the long-run production function is

$$Y(t) = AK(t) \tag{4.1}$$

where $K(t)$ is now interpreted as a broad aggregate of physical and human capital and A is a fixed technology parameter. As before, the model is driven by a capital accumulation function

$$\dot{K} = sAK - \delta K \tag{4.2}$$

where s is the savings rate and δ is the rate of physical capital depreciation. Capital per worker is $k(t) = K(t)/L(t)$ and the growth rate of the work force equals the growth rate of the population, so that $\dot{L}/L = n > 0$. The dynamics for capital per worker is then

$$\frac{\partial k}{\partial t} = \frac{\dot{K}}{L} - \frac{K}{L}\frac{\dot{L}}{L} = sAk - \delta k - nk \tag{4.3}$$

Output per worker is $y = AK/L = Ak$ and its growth rate is

$$\frac{\dot{y}}{y} = \frac{\dot{k}}{k} = sA - \delta - n \tag{4.4}$$

The key thing to notice in this expression is that any change in policy-related parameters like s and n will now have permanent effects on the growth rate. For instance, an increase in savings rate s will lead to a permanently higher growth rate. This result stands in contrast to predictions from the Solow model (see (3.7), where an increase in s only had a transitory effect on growth rates). A drawback is of course that the factors that drive long-run growth are still exogenous to the model.

4.3   Endogenous technological change

So far, we have basically neglected the issue of how technological progress comes about. In the Solow framework above, we simply assumed an exogenous growth rate g. It is well known that most of the progress in technological knowledge during the last century has been the result of intentional actions by scientists and engineers in large R&D departments within profit-maximizing firms. The famous models by Romer (1990) and Aghion and Howitt (1992) provided pioneering attempts to illustrate the mechanisms in this process. The subsection below presents a simplified version of those models.

4.3.1   An R&D sector

A key feature of the later endogenous growth models is the modeling of a separate R&D sector to which factors of production (mainly labor) are devoted on purpose. Let us assume that there are two sectors in the economy: a *final goods sector*, producing all the normal final goods and services that make up a country's GDP, and an *R&D sector*, producing new ideas or new technological knowledge that can be used in the final goods sector. The production function for the final goods sector is

$$Y(t) = A(t)(1-a)L(t) \tag{4.5}$$

where $A(t)$ is the level of technological knowledge at time t as before and a is the fraction of the total labor force $L(t)$ that is active in the R&D sector. A fraction $1 - a$ of total labor is thus left for the final goods sector.

The R&D sector has the production function

$$\dot{A}(t) = B(aL(t))^\gamma A(t)^\theta \tag{4.6}$$

where $B > 0$ is a parameter indicating the efficiency of research, $\gamma \in (0, 1)$ shows the output elasticity of labor in research, and $\theta \le 1$ is a parameter describing the elasticity of existing knowledge $A(t)$ for the production of increases in the stock of knowledge, $\dot{A}$. For simplicity, physical capital is now left out the model.

Two things are particularly noteworthy about equations (4.5) and (4.6). Firstly, A is available to the full amount in both sectors. The reason for this assumption is that ideas are inherently *nonrival* in character, i.e. one person's use of an idea (for instance, the blueprint for a new engine) does not preclude another person's simultaneous use of the same idea. Unlike ideas, most factors of production like capital and labor are *rival*, for instance in the sense that an actual engine can either be used in factory 1 or in factory 2, not in both at the same time. Labor is also a rival production factor since a fraction a is employed in R&D and $1 - a$ in the final goods sector.

Secondly, as we will see, the nature of the dynamics in this model will hinge on the level of the output elasticity of existing knowledge, θ. This parameter should be thought of as describing how useful older knowledge is for the creation of new knowledge. $\theta < 1$ implies that there is a kind of "fishing-out" effect in the sense that there are diminishing returns to the existing stock of technological knowledge in finding new ideas. We will return to this issue below.

A final assumption in the model is that labor grows at a rate $n > 0$ as before.

4.3.2 Steady-state equilibrium

From (4.6), we know that the growth rate of technological knowledge $g_A(t)$ will be equal to

$$\frac{\dot{A}}{A} = g_A(t) = Ba^\gamma L^\gamma A^{\theta-1} = \frac{Ba^\gamma L(t)^\gamma}{A(t)^{1-\theta}} \tag{4.7}$$

As in the Solow model, a balanced, steady-state growth rate will exist when $g_A(t)$ is constant over time, i.e. when $\frac{\partial g_A(t)}{\partial t} = \dot{g}(t) = 0$. From inspection of (4.7), we know that this will only happen if $L(t)^\gamma$ grows at the same rate as $A(t)^{1-\theta}$. One way of finding this level is to start by assuming that $\dot{g}_A = 0$. The time derivative of the growth rate in (4.7) is most easily found by first taking logs,

$$\ln g_A = \ln B + \gamma \ln(aL) + (\theta - 1) \ln A$$

and then taking the time derivative of the log:[1]

$$\frac{\partial \ln g_a}{\partial t} = \frac{\dot{g}_A}{g_A} = \gamma \frac{\dot{L}}{L} + (\theta - 1)\frac{\dot{A}}{A} = \gamma n + (\theta - 1)g_A$$

Multiplying this expression by g_A, and inserting the requirement that $\dot{g}_A = 0$ at the steady-state growth rate g_A^*, gives us

$$\dot{g}_A = [\gamma n + (\theta - 1)g_A^*]g_A^* = 0 \tag{4.8}$$

It is clear that this expression can only be zero if $g_A^* = 0$ or if $\gamma n + (\theta - 1)g_A^* = 0$. What type of equilibrium we will have will thus crucially depend on the level of θ.

In the case where $\theta = 1$, so that there are no diminishing returns to existing knowledge, as assumed in the original models of Romer (1990) and Aghion and Howitt (1992), the expression in the square brackets in (4.8) will not be zero and the only existing steady state in the current setting is $g_A^* = 0$. Note also that the (positive) growth rate of technological knowledge in this case will be $g_A(t) = B(aL)^\gamma$. An increase in the R&D labor force aL, caused by increases in either the share a or the size of the total labor force L, will thus increase the growth rate of technology. There will further never be a stagnation in growth rates.

In the case where $\theta < 1$, on the other hand, (4.8) will be satisfied if

$$\gamma n + (\theta - 1)g_A^* = 0 \Longrightarrow \gamma n = (1 - \theta)g_A^*$$

$$\Longrightarrow g_A^* = \frac{\gamma n}{1 - \theta}$$

A steady-state growth rate thus exists and will not depend on the level of the R&D labor force. This "semi-endogenous" growth result, due to Jones (1995), is thus free of the *scale effect* of R&D labor inherent in Romer (1990) and Aghion and Howitt (1992). Instead, only the growth rate of the population n will matter in the long run. Since output per capita equals $Y/L = A(1 - a)$, g_A^* will also be the growth rate of GDP per capita.

4.3.3   Allocation of labor

So far, we have said nothing about a, the proportion of labor employed in each sector. How should labor be allocated in equilibrium? As usual, if we assume competitive labor markets and freely mobile labor, workers should reallocate between sectors until they earn the same wage.

More formally, let us think of the final goods sector as being run by a single representative firm selling final goods at a price equal to unity and with profits given by

$$\Pi^F = A(1 - a)L - w(1 - a)L$$

The typical R&D firm, in turn, also only uses labor and has a profit function of the form

$$\Pi^R = P^A B (aL)^\gamma A^\theta - waL$$

where P^A is the price of the innovations that the R&D firm produces. For now, we will take that price as exogenously given. The first-order conditions for profit maximization give us

$$\frac{\partial \Pi^F}{\partial a} = -AL + wL = 0$$

$$\frac{\partial \Pi^R}{\partial a} = \gamma P^A B a^{\gamma-1} L^\gamma A^\theta - wL = 0$$

In equilibrium, the wage costs of the two firms should thus be the same. The conditions above imply that

$$\gamma P^A B a^{\gamma-1} L^\gamma A^\theta = AL$$

Using this term, we can solve for the optimal sectoral allocation a^*:

$$\left(a^*\right)^{\gamma-1} = \frac{A^{1-\theta} L^{1-\gamma}}{\gamma P^A B} \implies$$

$$a^* = \left(\frac{A^{1-\theta} L^{1-\gamma}}{\gamma P^A B}\right)^{\frac{1}{\gamma-1}} = \left(\frac{\gamma P^A B}{A^{1-\theta}}\right)^{\frac{1}{1-\gamma}} \frac{1}{L}$$

Given that $\gamma < 1$, the allocation of labor to R&D should thus increase with the price of innovations P^A and with R&D productivity B and decrease with L. The reason for the last observation is that workers face diminishing returns in the R&D sector, whereas we assume here constant returns in the final goods sector. Since we assume that L grows with an assumed rate of $n > 0$, this should imply that the share of workers in R&D should fall with time. Similarly, if $\theta < 1$ so that there are diminishing returns to the existing stock of technological knowledge, then a^* decreases with A. Note, however, that if $\theta = 1$ as in the steady-state result above, then a^* will be independent of the level of knowledge.

One of the key points with the result above is that a^* will be a positive function of the price of innovations P^A. But how is that price determined if ideas are a nonrival good? Fundamentally, the price of patents will depend on the institutions in society for intellectual property rights. If such property rights are weak, the price will be low and there will be weak incentives for people and firms to engage in R&D. On the positive side, without property rights to ideas, there would be no monopoly power for users of a particular innovation and anyone could commercialize any existing technological idea. According to the model, however, as

P^A goes to zero, a^* will also tend towards zero, so that no new ideas would be produced.

In the next section, we will extend the model and show how the price of innovations is determined in a market with monopolistic intermediate goods producers who buy patents on innovations from an R&D sector.

4.4   Romer's product variety model

In this section, we will recapitulate some of the details of the model in Romer (1990). The aim is to get a better understanding of what determines the price of innovations P^A and how the particular market structure with monopolistic intermediate goods firms affects the model. We will make the simplifying assumption that labor is only used in the final goods sector.[2]

4.4.1   Three sectors

The model assumes that there are three sectors:

- A final goods sector that employs all L workers as well as intermediate capital goods as factors of production.
- An intermediate goods sector using no labor but producing intermediate goods that are used as factors of production (physical capital) in the final goods sector. The patents for the intermediate goods are bought from the R&D sector and each intermediate goods producer is a monopolist on the good that they have acquired a patent on.
- An R&D sector that produces patents for intermediate goods and sells them to the intermediate goods producers.

Final goods (equivalent to total measured output in the economy) are produced by a representative firm according to the function

$$Y = L^{1-\alpha} \sum_{j=1}^{A} (X_j)^\alpha = L^{1-\alpha}(X_1^\alpha + X_2^\alpha + \cdots + X_A^\alpha) \tag{4.9}$$

where X_j is the amount of an intermediate capital good of vintage j (one might, for instance, think of X_j as the quantity of machine j). Let us for simplicity assume that L is now a constant. There are $A > 0$ intermediate goods in the economy. The number of intermediate goods is equivalent to the level of technology in this model. A noteworthy feature of the production function (4.9) is that marginal products of the intermediate goods are all given by

$$\frac{\partial Y}{\partial X_j} = \alpha L^{1-\alpha} X_j^{\alpha-1} \quad \text{for all } j \tag{4.10}$$

The marginal product of good j is thus independent of the levels of all other intermediate goods. One might think of the intermediate goods in the model as major inventions that are neither substitutes for nor complements to each other. The price of final goods is assumed to be 1.

The representative final goods producer maximizes profits:

$$\max_X \Pi^F = L^{1-\alpha} \sum_{j=1}^{A} (X_j)^{\alpha} - \sum_{j=1}^{A} P_j X_j$$

where P_j is the price of intermediate good j. The usual first-order conditions yield

$$\frac{\partial \Pi^F}{\partial X_j} = \alpha L^{1-\alpha} X_j^{\alpha-1} - P_j = 0 \tag{4.11}$$

Condition (4.11) states the familiar result that firms should acquire capital good j up to the level where its value marginal product equals its marginal cost, which is P_j. Equation (4.11) can be rewritten so as to obtain an expression for the final goods sector's demand for good j:

$$X_j = \left(\frac{\alpha}{P_j} \right)^{\frac{1}{1-\alpha}} L \tag{4.12}$$

Demand increases linearly with the work force but decreases, as expected, with the price charged by the intermediate firm.

Each intermediate good is produced by a single intermediate goods producer who has a patent on the good in question for a period of T years and hence a monopoly on its production. No labor is used in this sector. The marginal cost of producing one unit of good j is simply assumed to be equal to 1. The profit function is therefore given by

$$\Pi_j^I = (P_j - 1) X_j (P_j) \tag{4.13}$$

This expression contains the usual trade-off for a price-setting monopolist: revenues are increased directly by an increase in P_j but demand falls since $X_j'(P_j) < 0$. As will be apparent later, it is convenient at this stage to calculate the price elasticity of demand, i.e. the increase in demand from a marginal increase in price, multiplied by the ratio of the price to the level of demand:

$$X_j'(P_j) \frac{P_j}{X_j(P_j)} = - \frac{\alpha^{\frac{1}{1-\alpha}} L}{(1-\alpha) P_j^{\frac{1}{1-\alpha}+1}} \frac{P_j}{X_j(P_j)}$$

$$= - \frac{X_j(P_j)}{(1-\alpha) P_j} \frac{P_j}{X_j(P_j)} = - \frac{1}{1-\alpha}$$

The price elasticity of demand is thus negative and constant regardless of the level of demand.

The profit-maximizing price is obtained by taking the first-order condition for maximum:

$$\frac{\partial \Pi_j^I}{\partial P_j} = X_j(P_j) + P_j X_j'(P_j) - X_j'(P_j) = 0$$

This is a typical first-order condition for a monopolistic firm. We can rearrange this condition as $X_j(P_j) = X_j'(P_j)(1 - P_j)$ and then multiply both sides by $P_j / X_j(P_j)$ to obtain

$$P_j = X_j'(P_j) \frac{P_j}{X_j(P_j)}(1 - P_j) = -\frac{1}{1 - \alpha}(1 - P_j)$$

Note that we have inserted the derived expression for the price elasticity of demand on the right-hand side. By rearranging the last equation so as to isolate P_j, we finally obtain the profit-maximizing price for the monopolist and the corresponding level of demand from the final goods sector and profits for the intermediate goods sector:

$$P_j^* = \frac{1}{\alpha}$$

Since $\alpha < 1$, we can infer that $P_j^* > 1$, i.e. the monopolistic intermediate goods producer will charge a price higher than the marginal cost, which is equal to 1. In microeconomics textbooks, this phenomenon is known as *mark-up pricing*.[3]

When we have solved for P_j^*, the corresponding equilibrium levels of final sector demand and intermediate sector profits can be derived to be

$$X_j(P_j^*) = \alpha^{\frac{2}{1-\alpha}} L, \quad \Pi_j^I = (P_j^* - 1)X_j(P_j^*) = (1 - \alpha)\alpha^{\frac{1+\alpha}{1-\alpha}} L \qquad (4.14)$$

Note that the solution in (4.14) implies that $X_j(P_j^*) = X_{j+1}(P_{j+1}^*) = \cdots = X_A(P_A^*)$. Hence, we can express the equilibrium level of total output of final goods in (4.9) without a summation sign and instead multiply the solution for $X_j(P_j^*)$ by A to obtain

$$Y^* = L^{1-\alpha} A\alpha^{\frac{2}{1-\alpha}} L = A\alpha^{\frac{2}{1-\alpha}} L^{2-\alpha} \qquad (4.15)$$

In accordance with intuition, total output of final goods therefore increases with the number of intermediate goods A, which in this model is an indicator of the state of technological knowledge.

Finally, then, we can describe the R&D sector that produces patents and sells them to intermediate goods producers. The patentable invention of one additional design for a new intermediate good is made using a production function $BA(t)$, where B is a productivity parameter as before and A is the existing stock of patents at time t. The output is certain and always results in a new design that can be patented.[4] As before, we assume that knowledge about previous patents is fully accessible to the R&D firm. $A(t)$ is thus a nonrival production factor since it is available to the full extent both in the final goods sector and in the R&D sector, although it is partially excludable since only one intermediate goods producer has a patent and is allowed to produce the patented good commercially. There is free entry into the sector.

If the R&D firm chooses to make the invention, this will entail a fixed cost $\eta > 0$. As we shall see, this fixed cost will be very important for the determination of the price P_j^A that the R&D firm charges for the invention.

4.4.2 Solving the model in two stages

In order to find the optimal price P_j^A, we must first note that it is not obvious that the R&D firm will choose to invent a new design at all. A necessary condition is that $P_j^A \geq \eta$. If not, then the R&D firm is better off if it does not produce at all. P_j^A will of course also depend on the intermediate goods sector's willingness to pay.

The problem can be solved by thinking of it as a two-stage procedure:

- *First stage*: The R&D firm decides on whether to invent a new good or not.
- *Second stage*: Once the new good has been invented, the R&D firm decides on what price P_j^A to charge the intermediate goods producing firm j for the patent. The intermediate firm produces the good and it is sold to the final goods sector, where it is used in the production of final goods.

As is standard in this type of two-stage analysis, we use backward induction and start at the second stage. Given that the R&D firm has decided to come up with a new patent idea, what price should it charge for the patent? This will of course depend on the value of the patent for the intermediate firm. The intermediate goods producer can use the patent for T years and hence earn monopoly profits throughout this period. The equilibrium profits of the intermediate goods producer are given by (4.14). Such profits can be made for T years. The value of the firm, which we can refer to as V_j, is the discounted value of all future profits until the patent expires:

$$V_j(0) = \sum_{t=0}^{T} \Pi_j^I \beta^t = (1-\alpha)\alpha^{\frac{1+\alpha}{1-\alpha}} L \sum_{t=0}^{T} \beta^t \tag{4.16}$$

where $\beta \leq 1$ is a time discount factor. Clearly, the lower is β, the lower is the present value of the firm. If we make the greatly simplifying assumption that $\beta = 1$, then $V_j(0) = T(1-\alpha)\alpha^{\frac{1+\alpha}{1-\alpha}} L$.

The R&D firm observes the intermediate goods firm's value function and will bid up the price of the patent until $P_j^A = V_j(0)$. A higher price $P_j^A > V_j(0)$ is not possible; in that case the intermediate goods producer will not buy the patent. The R&D firm will thus squeeze out all the profits that the intermediate goods firm can make.

There must also be equilibrium in the capital market. In buying the patent, the intermediate firm makes an investment of size P_j^A. During a given time period, the returns to this investment must not be less than the returns that the firm could have received by investing in a risk-free asset at an interest rate $r > 0$. Hence, in equilibrium it must be the case that $rP_j^A = \Pi_j^I$.

In a general equilibrium model, there must be equilibria on all markets. In the R&D sector, finally, if $P_j^A > \eta$, then new R&D firms will enter the sector and squeeze down profits. Hence, an equilibrium price will require that $P_j^A = \eta$. In this case, the typical R&D firm will still choose to invent in the first stage and all the other things will happen in the second stage.

The conditions above imply that we can write

$$r = \frac{\Pi_j^I}{P_j^A} = \frac{(1-\alpha)\alpha^{\frac{1+\alpha}{1-\alpha}} L}{\eta} \tag{4.17}$$

We will return to this result below.

To close the model, note that the market value of all firms in the economy at time 0 is

$$\sum_{j=1}^{A(0)} \Pi_j^I = A(0)T(1-\alpha)\alpha^{\frac{1+\alpha}{1-\alpha}} L$$

The aggregate market value will increase linearly with the number of existing inventions A, with the duration of patents T, and with the size of the labor force L. That market value increases with the number of inventions (and hence of intermediate goods producers) is not surprising. The market value increases also with L. The reason is that the demand for intermediate capital goods in the final goods sector increases linearly with L. More workers means that the marginal product of a new machine is high and hence that demand for that machine is high.

T might be thought of here as the strength of intellectual property rights, where a large T means strong rights.[5] What would happen in our model if the strength of such rights suddenly fell? In the short run, this would cause a disequilibrium, which would lead to a number of responses. To start with, the market value of firms $V_j(0)$ would fall. This would in turn mean that the price for patents charged by the R&D sector P_j^A would be too high for the intermediate goods producers. In the short run, R&D firms will therefore choose not to produce any new inventions and exit from the sector. A new equilibrium can only be restored if also the fixed costs of invention η fall.

A value of $T = 0$ would be equivalent to saying that intellectual property rights do not exist. In such a world, any intermediate goods producing firm can use any invention without paying for it and there would be no monopolies and no mark-up pricing. This might have positive welfare effects in the short run since it implies a lower price of intermediate goods (it would fall from $1/\alpha$ to 1, i.e. the marginal cost of production in (4.13)) and total demand would increase from $\alpha^{\frac{2}{1-\alpha}} L$ to L (since $\alpha = 1$). Total output would also increase to $Y = A\alpha^{\frac{1}{1-\alpha}} L^{2-\alpha} = AL$. However, on the downside, A would cease to grow in our model, since as long there is some positive cost of invention $\eta > 0$, there is no incentive whatsoever to produce new ideas that cannot be sold. The issue of whether intellectual property rights is a good or a bad thing thus entails a trade-off in the model as outlined here; the absence of property rights removes monopolies and increases welfare in the short run but decreases the production of inventions in the long run.

4.5 Schumpeterian growth models

In Romer's model, each new intermediate good makes a positive contribution to the overall economy and total output in (4.15) increases linearly with A. Intermediate goods producers never really go out of business since there is always a demand for the good that they are producing.

Building on the classical works of Josef Schumpeter (1934), Aghion and Howitt (1992) outline a model with the same basic features as in Romer (1990) but with the important difference that there is instead a fixed number of goods to be produced and that firms compete over quality. As soon as a firm comes up with a new and better version of the good, this firm will take the whole market and render all older versions obsolete. Even though the "incumbent", leading firm in the sector had a monopoly, this now becomes useless. In the literature, this is referred to as *business stealing*.

Schumpeter recognized already in the early 1900s that entrepreneurs in modern capitalism had this inherent tendency of not only bringing forth new products but also continuously destroying a large share of rents for the existing firms. He famously referred to this phenomenon as *creative destruction*.

In Aghion and Howitt's (1992) model, total output is given by

$$Y = L^{1-\alpha} \sum_{j=1}^{N} (q^{\lambda_j} X_j)^{\alpha} = L^{1-\alpha}[(q^{\lambda_1} X_1)^{\alpha} + (q^{\lambda_2} X_2)^{\alpha} + \cdots + (q^{\lambda_N} X_N)^{\alpha}]$$

(4.18)

Just like before, L is the total labor force and X_j is the the quantity used of the intermediate capital good j. $N > 0$ is now the fixed number of intermediate goods in the economy. The key new feature of this production function is the inclusion of a quality indicator q^{λ_j}, where $q > 1$ and the exponent $\lambda_j \geq 1$ is a discrete number 1, 2, 3, ... reflecting how many times that sector j has undergone innovation. For simplicity, it is assumed that in each sector, each new innovation improves quality by a factor of q. Different sectors might have had different innovation intensity so that, for instance, it is possible that $\lambda_j > \lambda_{j+1}$. As has probably become evident, λ_j is now our indicator of technological progress.

The other key difference is that a new superior innovation in sector j is assumed to appear after $T_{\lambda_j} \geq 1$ periods. T_{λ_j} is now random and takes on a value $1, 2, 3, \ldots$ with a certain probability distribution.[6] When a new innovation of quality $q^{\lambda_j+1} > q^{\lambda_j}$ then appears, the existing monopoly ends. The firm is assumed to be risk-neutral and does not take any extra precautions due to this risk.

Apart from these two new assumptions, the model has the same structure as in Romer (1990). It can be solved by following the same steps as above. Since intermediate firms are monopolists, they will charge a mark-up price $P_j^* = 1/\alpha$. Through the usual profit-maximization conditions, final sector demand for the most recent version of good j can be shown to be $X_j^* = L\alpha^{\frac{2}{1-\alpha}} q^{\frac{\alpha\lambda_j}{1-\alpha}}$, which is the same expression as in (4.14) except that it is multiplied by $q^{\frac{\alpha\lambda_j}{1-\alpha}}$. Note that final sector demand thus increases with quality. Since the price is the same as before, this is not surprising.

Let us assume that the R&D firm has come up with a new innovation at time 0 and that the intermediate firm considers whether to buy the patent or not. The expected discounted value of the intermediate firm at time 0 would then be

$$E_0(V_j) = \sum_{t=0}^{E_0(T_{\lambda_j})} \Pi_j^I \beta^t = (1-\alpha)L\alpha^{\frac{1+\alpha}{1-\alpha}} q^{\frac{\alpha\lambda_j}{1-\alpha}} \sum_{t=0}^{E_0(T_{\lambda_j})} \beta^t$$

The noteworthy features of this expression are the two terms $q^{\frac{\alpha\lambda_j}{1-\alpha}}$ and $E_0(T_{\lambda_j})$. Rapid technological progress in this model means that a relatively large number of innovations happen all the time. On the one hand, this means that at time 0, λ_j should be relatively large, which would imply a relatively high $E_0(V_j)$. But on the other hand, rapid technological progress would also mean that the expected duration of monopoly should be short, i.e. $E_0(T_{\lambda_j})$ should be small and the expected value of the firm relatively small. If the latter effect dominates, firms will be discouraged from entering the sector. In this manner, creative destruction does not have an unambiguously positive effect on the economy.

4.6   Innovation versus imitation

The models reviewed so far in this chapter have all had developed rich countries in mind that have sufficient economic and human resources to engage in R&D that expands the world technological frontier. However, it is well known that most of the countries in the world do not pursue R&D at all but rather aim to imitate the innovations developed elsewhere. In this section, we will briefly present a model that considers the choice between innovation and imitation along the lines of Acemoglu et al (2003).

The basic idea in this model is that the level of technological knowledge in a country can be enhanced either by innovation or by imitation. The total level of effort in society is unity and an effort level $e < 1$ is devoted to imitation and $1 - e$ to innovation. Effort might in this setting be interpreted as working time or directed investments or policies pursued by the government. Innovation requires a relatively high level of skills, whereas imitation does not. Let us imagine that the level of technological knowledge in a country at time t is given by

$$A_t = e\mu \bar{A}_{t-1} + \gamma (1 - e) H_{t-1} A_{t-1} \qquad (4.19)$$

The current level of technology A_t is thus a result of a process exploiting last year's level of knowledge in the country A_{t-1} as well as the level at the world technology frontier, $\bar{A}_{t-1}$. The two terms are multiplied respectively by effort levels and the parameters $\mu, \gamma > 0$ that describe the (time-invariant) usefulness of imitation and innovation for knowledge growth in the country. Furthermore, A_{t-1} is multiplied by the level of human capital H_{t-1}, capturing the general level of education in the country. This reflects the assumption that innovation is inherently more reliant on skills than imitation.[7]

If we divide expression (4.19) by A_{t-1} and subtract $A_{t-1}/A_{t-1} = 1$ on both sides, we can write

$$\frac{A_t - A_{t-1}}{A_{t-1}} = g_{t-1} = e\mu d_{t-1} + \gamma (1 - e) H_{t-1} - 1$$

where $d_{t-1} = \bar{A}_{t-1}/A_{t-1} \geq 1$ is a measure of the country's distance from the world technological frontier. If d_{t-1} is large, imitation is relatively effective.

How should a social planner in a country optimally devote effort to imitation and innovation? The simple answer is that all effort should be devoted to imitation if the marginal product of imitation exceeds the marginal product of innovation, i.e. if $\mu d_{t-1} > \gamma H_{t-1}$, and to innovation if the opposite result holds. The main insight from this expression is that in countries that are far from the technological frontier (a high d_{t-1}) and where human capital levels are relatively low, the growth of technological knowledge is optimally driven solely by imitation and is given by $g_{t-1} = \mu d_{t-1} - 1$. On the other hand, for countries at the technological frontier where $d_{t-1} = 1$, it will be the case that imitation is not possible, that the optimal level of imitation effort is $e = 0$, and that $g_{t-1} = \gamma H_{t-1} - 1$. Note also that if the level of human capital were a choice variable for governments, it would in this model be pointless to increase, for instance, levels of engineering skills (H_{t-1}) if the country is mainly an imitator, since such skills are only useful for innovation.

5 The Overlapping Generations Model

The growth models presented so far were representations of how macro variables and profit-maximizing firms are hypothesized to behave in relation to each other. None of the results were based on an analysis of household behavior over time, i.e. on the behavior of and choices made by utility-maximizing individuals and households who live for more than one period and who care about the future. The overlapping generations (OLG) model outlined below now introduces a micro-founded model of economic growth and intertemporal choice that will be employed as a "workhorse" model in several chapters to follow.

One of the key advantages of the OLG model is that it allows us to derive an endogenous saving rate. In the Solow model, the saving rate s was simply exogenously determined.

The OLG model was initially presented by Diamond (1965) and Blanchard (1985). We will henceforth carry out the analysis in *discrete time*, i.e. we consider periods $t, t+1, t+2, \ldots$, instead of a continuous time framework. As we shall see, the insights from a discrete time framework are complementary to those already shown.

5.1 Household optimization

The model makes the following basic assumptions. Individuals live for two periods. In the first period of an individual's life, he or she belongs to a *young* generation and in the second generation to an *old* generation. In each period, there is a young and an old generation living at the same time (hence the term "overlapping generations"). Let us denote consumption by an individual in generation j during period t as $c_{j,t}$, where $j = 1$ means the young generation and $j = 2$ means the old generation and $t = 1, 2, 3, \ldots$ is the actual period in question.[1] Individuals are born without any assets except 1 unit of labor supply. We assume that people gain utility only from their own consumption and that they do not leave any money for future generations.

In the most general case, let us write the utility function for an individual who is young in period t as

$$U_t = u(c_{1,t}) + \beta u(c_{2,t+1}) \tag{5.1}$$

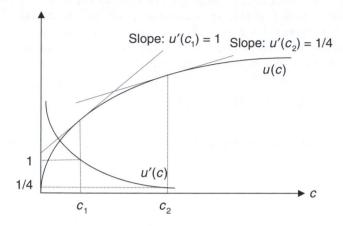

Figure 5.1 A strictly concave utility function and its associated marginal utility.

where $\beta \leq 1$ is a time discount factor. The closer β is to unity, the greater the patience of individuals. If β instead is very low, the individual discounts the future a lot and thinks consumption when young is more valuable in relative terms. The utility function satisfies the usual assumptions of a positive but strictly diminishing marginal utility, so that $u'(c_{j,t}) > 0$ and $u''(c_{j,t}) < 0$ at all $c_{j,t} > 0$. It is further *time-separable* since $u'(c_{1,t})$ is independent of $c_{2,t+1}$.

The utility function and its associated marginal utility curve are shown in Figure 5.1. In order to understand more intuitively how the curves are linked, consider for instance the point on $u(c)$ where the slope is equal to unity. The level of c at which this happens is $c = c_1$ so that $u'(c_1) = 1$. At some higher level of c, for instance at $c = c_2 > c_1$, we have that $u'(c_2) = 1/4 < u'(c_1)$. It is important to understand this basic theme of utility functions because it will appear again and again in this text: as c increases, $u(c)$ increases whereas $u'(c)$ falls.

Individuals earn an income $y_{1,t}$ during young age in period t and an income $y_{2,t+1}$ when they are old. What is not consumed in the first period can be saved for old age. The individual will then get an interest rate r_{t+1} on their savings, which amount to $s_t = y_{1,t} - c_{1,t} \geq 0$. However, savings may also be negative, such that $s_t = y_{1,t} - c_{1,t} < 0$. In that case individuals borrow for consumption in the first period at the same interest rate r_{t+1}.[2] Consumption during old age is thus

$$c_{2,t+1} = y_{2,t+1} + (y_{1,t} - c_{1,t})(1 + r_{t+1}) \tag{5.2}$$

If we isolate the income terms on the right-hand side, we get what is usually referred to as the individual's *intertemporal budget constraint*:

$$\frac{c_{2,t+1}}{(1 + r_{t+1})} + c_{1,t} = \frac{y_{2,t+1}}{(1 + r_{t+1})} + y_{1,t} \tag{5.3}$$

What this expression says is that the present value of a person's current and future consumption must be equal to the present value of his or her lifetime incomes.[3]

How much should the individual optimally consume in each period? In order to solve this problem, we can start by inserting (5.2) into the utility function in (5.1) and take the first-order condition for a maximum:

$$\frac{\partial U_t}{\partial c_{1,t}} = u'(c_{1,t}) - \beta u'(c_{2,t+1})(1 + r_{t+1}) = 0$$

By rewriting this expression, we obtain what is usually referred to as the *Euler equation*:

$$\frac{u'(c_{1,t}^*)}{u'(c_{2,t+1}^*)} = \beta(1 + r_{t+1}) \tag{5.4}$$

This fundamental result will be derived many times in the chapters to come. It implies that an individual should optimally consume so that the relative marginal utility of consumption when young, $u'(c_{1,t}^*)/u'(c_{2,t+1}^*)$, exactly equals $\beta(1 + r_{t+1})$, where $c_{j,t}^*$ denotes an optimal level. What does this imply for the optimal relative level of consumption $c_{1,t}^*/c_{2,t+1}^*$?

Consider, for instance, a case where individuals are patient so that β is close to unity and where r_{t+1} is relatively high. In that case, it is likely that $\beta(1 + r_{t+1}) > 1$. According to (5.4), we must then optimally have chosen consumption levels such that $u'(c_{1,t}^*)/u'(c_{2,t+1}^*) > 1$ applies as well. Note that $u'(c_{1,t}^*) > u'(c_{2,t+1}^*)$ must (due to diminishing marginal utility as illustrated in Figure 5.1) imply that $c_{1,t}^* < c_{2,t+1}^*$. Hence, if individuals are patient and if interest rates are high, consumption should be greater in old age than during youth, and vice versa.

With a general utility function like that in (5.1), we cannot get any further than interpreting the optimality condition in (5.4). We are not able get any explicit solution for either $c_{1,t}^*$, $c_{2,t+1}^*$, or the level of saving. If we want to achieve closed-form solutions, we need to assume a more specific utility function.

5.1.1   *Example 1: Logarithmic utility*

One of the very simplest cases is to assume logarithmic utility such that $u(c_{j,t}) = \ln c_{j,t}$. Logarithmic utility implies that the utility function is concave and that the individual is risk-averse, since $u'(c_{j,t}) = 1/c_{j,t} > 0$ and $u''(c_{j,t}) = -1/c_{j,t}^2 < 0$. The Euler condition (5.4) then simply becomes

$$\frac{c_{2,t+1}^*}{c_{1,t}^*} = \beta(1 + r_{t+1}) \tag{5.5}$$

From this condition, we can achieve closed-form solutions for our intertemporal choice of consumption. Insert $c_{2,t+1}^* = \beta(1 + r_{t+1})c_{1,t}^*$ into the left-hand side of (5.2) and solve for $c_{1,t}^*$ to find

$$c_{1,t}^* = \frac{y_{2,t+1} + y_{1,t}(1 + r_{t+1})}{(1 + \beta)(1 + r_{t+1})}$$

When we have solved for $c_{1,t}$, it is of course easy to also solve for $c_{2,t+1}$:

$$c_{2,t+1}^* = \frac{\beta[y_{2,t+1} + y_{1,t}(1 + r_{t+1})]}{1 + \beta}$$

These results have some straightforward interpretations. First, optimal consumption in both periods increase with income levels $y_{1,t}$ and $y_{2,t+1}$. Second, we already know from before that $c_{2,t+1}^*$ increases with people's patience β and with the interest rate r_{t+1}. However, note that an increase in r_{t+1} with incomes held constant will lower $c_{1,t}^*$. This might be referred to as a *substitution effect*: the individual substitutes consumption in young age for consumption in old age.

We can also solve for the optimal level of savings:

$$s_t^* = y_{1,t} - c_{1,t}^* = \frac{y_{1,t}\beta(1 + r_{t+1}) - y_{2,t+1}}{(1 + \beta)(1 + r_{t+1})}$$

Not surprisingly, savings increase with $y_{1,t}$, β and with r_{t+1}. Note, however, that, all else being equal, a net increase in $y_{2,t+1}$ will lead to a decrease in savings.

5.1.2 *Example 2: CRRA utility*

Let us now assume that the utility of an individual is given by a function characterized by constant relative risk aversion (CRRA) where $u(c_{j,t}) = (c_{1t}^{1-\theta} - 1)/(1 - \theta)$ and $\beta = 1/(1 + \rho) \leq 1$:

$$U_t = \frac{c_{1,t}^{1-\theta} - 1}{1 - \theta} + \frac{1}{1 + \rho}\frac{c_{2,t+1}^{1-\theta} - 1}{1 - \theta} \tag{5.6}$$

Here $\rho \geq 0$ is a time discount rate and θ is the Arrow–Pratt measure of relative risk aversion (individuals are risk-averse). The CRRA utility function is particularly useful since it can encompass several different types of utility, depending on the value of θ. A $\theta < 0$ means that the individual is risk-loving (since marginal utility $c^{-\theta}$ increases with the level of c), $\theta = 0$ means risk neutrality, whereas $\theta > 0$ implies a risk-averse individual. It can further be shown that if $\theta = 1$, then $u(c_{j,t}) = \ln c_{j,t}$.[4] The case most often studied will be $\theta \in (0, 1)$.

We now assume, for simplicity, that individuals earn a wage income when young, $y_{1,t} = w_t$, and that an old individual has zero income, $y_{2,t+1} = 0$. Hence, young individuals must save some of their labor income when young in order to consume when old:

$$s_t = w_t - c_{1,t} \tag{5.7}$$

When old, individuals consume their savings from the previous period plus the interest earned from these savings:

$$c_{2,t+1} = (1 + r_{t+1})s_t = (1 + r_{t+1})(w_t - c_{1,t}) \tag{5.8}$$

In this expression, r_{t+1} is the interest rate on savings as before.

The intertemporal budget constraint reduces to

$$c_{1,t} + \frac{c_{2,t+1}}{1 + r_{t+1}} = w_t \tag{5.9}$$

The objective function in (5.6) and the constraint in (5.9) define a constrained maximization problem, which can be solved by forming a Lagrangian function

$$\Gamma = \frac{c_{1,t}^{1-\theta} - 1}{1 - \theta} + \frac{1}{1 + \rho} \frac{c_{2,t+1}^{1-\theta} - 1}{1 - \theta} + \lambda \left(w_t - c_{1,t} - \frac{c_{2,t+1}}{1 + r_{t+1}} \right)$$

where λ is a Lagrange multiplier.[5]

The first-order conditions for c_{1t} and c_{2t+1} are

$$\frac{\partial \Gamma}{\partial c_{1,t}} = c_{1,t}^{-\theta} - \lambda = 0$$

$$\frac{\partial \Gamma}{\partial c_{2,t+1}} = \frac{c_{2,t+1}^{-\theta}}{1 + \rho} - \frac{\lambda}{(1 + r_{t+1})} = 0$$

Since $c_{1t}^{-\theta} = \lambda$ and $\frac{c_{2t+1}^{-\theta}(1 + r_{t+1})}{1 + \rho} = \lambda$, we can write

$$c_{1t}^{-\theta} = \frac{c_{2,t+1}^{-\theta}(1 + r_{t+1})}{1 + \rho} \implies \frac{c_{2,t+1}^*}{c_{1t}^*} = \left(\frac{1 + r_{t+1}}{1 + \rho} \right)^{\frac{1}{\theta}} = 1 + g_{c,t} \tag{5.10}$$

In other words, the relative consumption of the individual when in old age can be described as $1 + g_{c,t}$, where

$$g_{c,t} = \frac{c_{2,t+1} - c_{1t}}{c_{1t}} = \frac{(1 + r_{t+1})^{\frac{1}{\theta}} - (1 + \rho)^{\frac{1}{\theta}}}{(1 + \rho)^{\frac{1}{\theta}}}$$

is the growth rate of consumption between t and $t + 1$. Note that $g_{c,t}$ can be positive or negative. $g_{c,t}$ will depend positively on the interest rate r_{t+1}, negatively on the time discount rate ρ, and negatively on the risk-aversion parameter θ. The greater is ρ, the greater is the individual's impatience and hence the lower is their consumption when old. A θ that approaches 1 further means that the utility function has a markedly concave curvature and that the marginal utility of consumption diminishes fast ($\theta = 1$ implies that $u(c_{j,t}) = \ln c_{j,t}$). Such individuals will also consume relatively less in the future than if they entertained a θ that is close to 0.

The result in (5.10) is often referred to as the "discrete Ramsey" result.[6] It will play an important role in the sections ahead. Note that the requirement for a positive growth rate is that $r_{t+1} > \rho$. The next step is to derive an expression for r_{t+1}.

5.2 Endogenous saving

In this section, we will now extend the model to include factor markets. From (5.7), (5.8), and (5.10) we know that

$$\frac{c^*_{2,t+1}}{c^*_{1,t}} = \frac{(1+r_{t+1})s_t}{(w_t - s_t)} = 1 + g_{c,t}$$

which implies that

$$(1+r_{t+1})s_t + (1+g_{c,t})s_t = (1+g_{c,t})w_t$$

and that

$$s_t = \frac{(1+g_{c,t})w_t}{2+r_{t+1}+g_{c,t}} = \frac{w_t}{(1+r_{t+1})/(1+g_{c,t})+1}$$

Inserting the expression for $1 + g_{c,t}$ from (5.10) yields

$$s_t = \frac{w_t}{(1+r_{t+1})^{\frac{\theta-1}{\theta}}(1+\rho)^{\frac{1}{\theta}}+1} \tag{5.11}$$

Saving will thus be a positive function of w_t and of r_{t+1} (since $\theta < 1$). Both are unknown at this stage. However, by introducing firms into the analysis, we might also derive w_t and r_{t+1}. Not surprisingly, saving decreases with the time discount rate ρ.

5.2.1 *Firms*

Firms produce according to the standard neoclassical aggregate production function

$$Y_t = F(K_t, L), \quad \text{where} \quad \frac{Y_t}{L} = f(k_t) \quad \text{and} \quad Y_t = Lf(k_t)$$

We assume that labor and capital are paid their marginal products:

$$r_t = \frac{\partial Y_t}{\partial K_t} = L f'(k_t) \frac{1}{L} = f'(k_t)$$

$$w_t = \frac{\partial Y_t}{\partial L} = f(k_t) - L f'(k_t) \frac{K_t}{L^2} = f(k_t) - f'(k_t) k_t$$

Furthermore, the total capital stock at $t+1$ equals s_t (individual saving in period t) times the number of individuals L, so that $K_{t+1} = s_t L$.[7] This in turn implies that $k_{t+1} = s_t$.

5.2.2   The steady state

By inserting the derived terms for r_{t+1} and w_t into (5.11), taking into account that $k_{t+1} = s_t$, we can write

$$k_{t+1} = \frac{f(k_t) - f'(k_t) k_t}{[1 + f'(k_{t+1})]^{\frac{\theta-1}{\theta}} (1+\rho)^{\frac{1}{\theta}} + 1}$$

This expression is in general form and, although it shows k_{t+1} as a function of k_t, it is not very informative. We therefore make two additional assumptions: First, that the production function $f(k_t)$ is Cobb–Douglas, i.e. $f(k_t) = k^\alpha$. Second, in the utility function, we assume as before that $\theta = 1$ so that the utility function has a logarithmic form.

Armed with these two assumptions, the equation for k_{t+1} simplifies considerably:

$$k_{t+1} = \frac{k_t^\alpha - \alpha k_t^\alpha}{(1 + \alpha k_{t+1}^{\alpha-1})^0 (1+\rho)^1 + 1} = \frac{k_t^\alpha (1-\alpha)}{2+\rho} = s_t \qquad (5.12)$$

In a steady state, it must be the case that $k_{t+1} = k_t = k^* = s^*$. Thus

$$k^* = \frac{(k^*)^\alpha (1-\alpha)}{2+\rho} \implies k^* = \left(\frac{1-\alpha}{2+\rho}\right)^{\frac{1}{1-\alpha}}$$

Note that this is the equivalent of the steady-state level of k derived in the Solow model. The key difference is that ρ enters this expression since we have now explicitly taken into account an individual's preferences. k^* will decrease with ρ just like the growth rate of consumption in (5.10) decreases with ρ. Hence, the greater the individual's patience, the lower is ρ and the greater is the steady-state level of the capital stock. It is further easily derived that the equilibrium level of output per capita is $y^* = (k^*)^\alpha = (\frac{1-\alpha}{2+\rho})^{\frac{\alpha}{1-\alpha}}$.

5.3 Endogenous growth

A key result from the OLG model is that the optimal intertemporal growth rate of consumption is given by

$$\frac{c_{2t+1} - c_{1t}}{c_{1t}} = g_c^* = \left(\frac{1 + r_{t+1}}{1 + \rho}\right)^{\frac{1}{\theta}} - 1$$

In the OLG model, r_{t+1} was found as in the analysis above. Let us now assume instead a world that is described by Romer's R&D model in Section 4.4 with the only exception that we now also specify household optimizing behavior as in Section 5.1 of the OLG model. Recall from (4.17) that in a general equilibrium, the intermediate firm's annual level of profit Π_j^I from investing a sum P_j^A in buying a patent lasting for T years must be equal to the risk-free annual return in the capital market on that same investment rP_j^A. Remember further that the R&D firms will charge a price $P_j^A = \eta$ for the patents, where η is the cost of developing the patent. This general equilibrium implies

$$\Pi_j^I = (1 - \alpha)\alpha^{\frac{1+\alpha}{1-\alpha}} L = r P_j^A = r\eta$$

If we combine these expressions, we can substitute in r and express the steady-state growth rate of optimal consumption in the Romer model as

$$g_c^* = \left(\frac{1 + \frac{1}{\eta}(1 - \alpha)\alpha^{\frac{1+\alpha}{1-\alpha}} L}{1 + \rho}\right)^{\frac{1}{\theta}} - 1$$

The growth rate will increase with the number of workers L. As explained above, this "scale effect" in the Romer model arises since more workers means a greater demand for intermediate goods. The growth rate will fall with the cost of inventing new goods, η. As before, the growth rate decreases with the level of the behavioral parameters θ and ρ.

Note that the equation above further implies that $g_c^* > 0$ only if $\frac{1}{\eta}(1 - \alpha)$ $\alpha^{\frac{1+\alpha}{1-\alpha}} L > \rho$. If people are generally impatient so that ρ is high and if the cost of invention η is high, then this criterion for positive growth might not be satisfied. It further suggests that a certain population size is necessary for R&D to be a viable path to consumption growth.

Part II
The Short and Medium Run

6 Equilibrium Business Cycles

From the long run, we now move to the short and medium run, by which we will here mean time periods of less than five years. Long-run growth is the average growth rate over decades, but in the shorter run there can be substantial cyclical variations in GDP, referred to as *business cycles*. The theory of *real business cycles* (RBCs) is associated mainly with Kydland and Prescott (1982) and Long and Plosser (1983). See also the overview in Rebelo (2005).

Early RBC models were in part inspired by the empirical record showing that business cycles did not appear to follow any systematic cyclical patterns. There was also a dissatisfaction with the Keynesian type of explanations emphasizing market failures in the form of, for instance, wage rigidities. Keynesian theory further lacked a micro foundation, i.e. the modeling was not based on the decisions of optimizing individuals. The RBC models instead proposed a framework based on individual behavior where the engine of the cyclical behavior was *real* shocks, induced by technological change and government spending, for instance, rather than *nominal* or *monetary* effects as emphasized by Keynesian theory. A further difference from previous modeling was the introduction of leisure in the utility function of the individual. This novelty made it possible to derive implications for the intertemporal substitution of labor supply.

6.1 Technology shocks to production

Let us assume that aggregate output in the economy is produced according to the Cobb–Douglas production function

$$Y_t = K_t^{\alpha}(A_t L_t)^{1-\alpha} \tag{6.1}$$

where K_t is total physical capital, A_t is the level of technological knowledge, and L_t is labor. Let us further assume for simplicity that K_t is exogenous to the model so that $K_t = K$. Labor is given by $L_t = N_t l_t$, where N_t is the size of the working population and l_t is the number of working hours that each worker provides. For simplicity, $N_t = N$. The key determinant of L_t is thus l_t. These assumptions mean that we can rewrite (6.1) in log form as

$$\ln Y_t = \alpha \ln K + (1 - \alpha) \ln N + (1 - \alpha)(\ln l_t + \ln A_t) \quad (6.2)$$
$$= \Omega + (1 - \alpha)(\ln l_t + \ln A_t)$$

where Ω is the exogenous part. The sources of variation in output will therefore be working hours l_t and technology A_t.

The development of technological knowledge is assumed to follow the following process:

$$\ln A_t = \bar{A} + gt + \tilde{A}_t \quad (6.3)$$

In this expression, $\bar{A}$ is the initial level of technology, g is the trend growth rate of technological knowledge (as in the Solow model), t is time, and $\tilde{A}_t$ is a stochastic shock to the trend. More specifically, the stochastic component is given by

$$\tilde{A}_t = \rho_A \tilde{A}_{t-1} + \epsilon_t \quad (6.4)$$

where $\rho_A \in (0, 1)$ is a parameter indicating the persistence of past shocks for the current level of technology and ϵ_t is an error term such that $E(\epsilon_t) = 0$ for all t. A positive technology shock might, for instance, be the sudden appearance of a new and drastically improved computer program or a breakthrough in transportation technology. A negative technology shock to trend growth could arise if the implementation of some existing technology unexpectedly stalled during some period.

In technical terms, the process described above follows a first-order autoregressive process (AR(1)) since $\tilde{A}_t$ depends on the corresponding level one period before. Inserting (6.4) into (6.3) gives us

$$\ln A_t = \bar{A} + gt + \rho_A \tilde{A}_{t-1} + \epsilon_t$$

where it might be noted that the expected level is $E_t(\ln A_t) = \bar{A} + gt + \rho_A \tilde{A}_{t-1}$ and where the expected growth rate of A_t is thus g.

In order to see the effects on output, suppose, for instance, that a positive technology shock happens in period 1 so that $\epsilon_1 = \bar{\epsilon} > 0$ and that $\epsilon_2 = \epsilon_3 = 0$. Assume also that $\tilde{A}_0 = 0$. In that case, $\tilde{A}_1 = \bar{\epsilon}$ and $\tilde{A}_2 = \rho_A \bar{\epsilon}$. By period 3, we have $\tilde{A}_3 = \rho_A(\tilde{A}_2) = \rho_A^2 \bar{\epsilon}$. The level of technological knowledge is therefore $\ln A_3 = \bar{A} + 3g + \rho_A^2 \bar{\epsilon}$. The shock in period 1 is still felt in period 3 by an amount $\rho_A^2 \bar{\epsilon}$. As time goes by, the effects of the shock approach zero since $\rho_A < 1$.

Finally, comparing the level of total output in the economy with and without the shock, we can infer from (6.2) that the shock causes a cyclical upturn since total output in period 3 is higher than usual by an amount $(1 - \alpha)\rho_A^2 \bar{\epsilon} > 0$.

6.2 Labor demand

One of the key consequences of technology shocks is the impact they have on the labor market. Let us imagine a representative firm i in the economy that produces according to the production function in (6.1) and sells its good at a price P_t.[1] For simplicity, we will set price equal to unity so that $P_t = 1$. The labor market is competitive and workers are hired until the *marginal product of labor* equals the market wage rate, w_t. The profit function for the representative firm is

$$\Pi_t^i = (K_t^i)^\alpha (A_t L_t^i)^{1-\alpha} - w_t L_t^i - r_t K_t^i \tag{6.5}$$

where K_t^i is the physical capital held by firm i at time t, L_t^i is the labor employed by firm i, A_t is nonrival technology available to all firms, and r_t is the interest rate on capital.

The first-order condition for profit maximization for labor is

$$\frac{\partial \Pi_t^i}{\partial L_t^i} = (K_t^i)^\alpha A_t^{1-\alpha}(1-\alpha)(L_t^i)^{-\alpha} - w_t = 0$$

where the left-hand side in the middle expression is the marginal product of labor.[2] Rearranging terms gives us an expression for firm i's demand for labor, $L^{i,D}$:[3]

$$L_t^{i,D} = K_t^i \left(\frac{(1-\alpha)A_t^{1-\alpha}}{w_t} \right)^{\frac{1}{\alpha}} \tag{6.6}$$

What is immediately evident from this expression is that labor demand will increase with a positive technology shock that increases A_t. Analogously, a negative technology shock will decrease labor demand. Labor demand will also increase with the firm's stock of capital K_t^i since that increases the marginal product of labor.

RBC models assume a perfectly functioning economy where all markets are in equilibrium. Hence, an increase in labor demand should generally mean that aggregate employment (in terms of working hours l_t) should increase. In the empirical literature, the prediction about a positive relationship between technology shocks and employment has been extensively discussed.

6.3 Households

Labor supply is determined by the households and involves a trade-off. On the one hand, more work means more income and higher consumption. On the other hand, more work means less leisure, which is now assumed to be a part of the individual's utility function. The lifetime utility of an individual who lives for two periods and who receives utility from consumption and leisure is given by the function

$$U = U(c_1, c_2, 1 - l_1, 1 - l_2) \tag{6.7}$$
$$= \ln c_1 + b \ln(1 - l_1) + \beta[\ln c_2 + b \ln(1 - l_2)]$$

where c_t is consumption in period $t = \{0, 1\}$, l_t is working hours in period t, $b > 0$ is a parameter showing the relative weight given to leisure, and $\beta \leq 1$ is a time discount factor. For simplicity, we have normalized total working hours to unity, so that the amount of leisure equals $1 - l_t$.

First-period consumption might be saved for the second period and the individual works in both periods for a wage w_t. Second-period consumption must therefore equal savings plus second-period income from work:

$$c_2 = (1 + r)(w_1 l_1 - c_1) + w_2 l_2$$

The individual receives a (real) interest rate r on savings $(w_1 l_1 - c_1)$. Rewriting this condition yields an intertemporal budget constraint:

$$c_1 + \frac{c_2}{1 + r} = w_1 l_1 + \frac{w_2 l_2}{1 + r} \tag{6.8}$$

By utilizing (6.7) and (6.8), we can set up the individual's maximization problem as a Lagrangian:

$$\Gamma = \ln c_1 + b \ln(1 - l_1) + \beta[\ln c_2 + b \ln(1 - l_2)]$$
$$+ \lambda \left(w_1 l_1 + \frac{w_2 l_2}{1 + r} - c_1 - \frac{c_2}{1 + r} \right)$$

In this optimization problem, we let labor supply l_1 and l_2 be the choice variables. The first-order conditions are

$$\frac{\partial \Gamma}{\partial l_1} = -\frac{b}{(1 - l_1^*)} + \lambda w_1 = 0 \tag{6.9}$$

$$\frac{\partial \Gamma}{\partial l_2} = -\frac{b\beta}{(1 - l_2^*)} + \frac{\lambda w_2}{1 + r} = 0 \tag{6.10}$$

By isolating the λs on the right-hand sides in (6.9) and (6.10), we can write

$$\lambda = \frac{b}{(1 - l_1^*)w_1} = \frac{b\beta(1 + r)}{(1 - l_2^*)w_2}$$

If we cancel the bs, this can in turn be rewritten as

$$\frac{1 - l_1^*}{1 - l_2^*} = \frac{1}{(1 + r)\beta} \frac{w_2}{w_1} \tag{6.11}$$

What we have achieved in (6.11) is an expression for the utility-maximizing relative leisure in period 1. Since it is not possible to obtain explicit solutions for l_1^* and l_2^*, we have to base our analysis on (6.11).[4]

Let us assume that there will be a known fall in the relative wage w_2/w_1. Such a fall means that $(1 - l_1^*)/(1 - l_2^*)$ optimally must fall too, implying that relative labor supply l_1^*/l_2^* must rise. In other words, a fall in the relative wage in period 2 means that individuals will work more in period 1, thus causing a temporary increase in total output in (6.2).

As another example, consider an increase in the real interest rate r. Just as in the previous case, such an increase means that relative first-period labor supply l_1^*/l_2^* must increase. The intuition is that a rise r makes first-period labor income relatively more valuable (since only first-period consumption can be saved), which leads to an intertemporal substitution of labor supply towards more work in the first period. This rational response to a real shock also leads to a boom in the first-period total income Y_t.

As the examples above have indicated, RBC models are often too complex to be solved analytically. Therefore, scholars in this tradition use advanced methods of simulation where realistic parameter values are plugged in before a variation in some real variable is made.

7 Financial Crises

In real business cycle models of the basic kind as above, all markets work efficiently, including the financial market. According to that logic, there is therefore no point in modeling a separate financial sector. However, the deep financial crisis that hit the world economy in autumn 2008 seems not to lend much support to an efficient financial market hypothesis. A recurring feature of financial crises rather appears to be *bank runs*, i.e. that a large number of depositors withdraw their savings at the same time, potentially causing banks to become insolvent and collapse.[1] In some serious cases, this might even cause a systemic banking crisis when a country's whole banking system is close to collapse.[2] The macroeconomic consequences on, for instance, economic growth and fiscal balances are typically substantial and go beyond normal business cycle downturns (Reinhart and Rogoff 2009a, b).

In this section, we present a model of bank runs from Chang and Velasco (2001), who in turn build upon Diamond and Dybwig (1983). It is mainly meant to capture an "emerging market" with an open economy and a fairly advanced banking sector. Recent events suggest that it might also be used to describe the situation in, for instance, the United States.

7.1 Basic assumptions

Let us consider an open economy with a large number of identical agents. There is one good that can be freely traded on world markets and that can be used for consumption or for investment. The price of the consumption good on world markets is fixed and set to one (dollar) for simplicity. There are three time periods, $t = 0, 1, 2$. The model contains the following key components:

- Domestic individuals are born with an endowment of $e > 0$ dollars.
- Domestic individuals might invest one dollar in a risk-free investment project at time $t = 0$ that yields $r < 1$ at $t = 1$ and $R > 1$ at $t = 2$. The investment project is said to be *illiquid*, since an early liquidation at time 1 causes a loss of $1 - r$ dollars.
- Domestic individuals can invest or borrow money on an international capital market at a zero interest rate. The maximum amount of borrowing is $f > 0$, which might be thought of as a domestically imposed credit restriction.

- Individuals are either "impatient" with a probability ρ and consume only in period 1 or "patient" with a probability $1 - \rho$ and derive utility only from consuming in period 2. The realization of each individual's type is private information.
- c_1 denotes consumption in period 1 if the individual turns out to be impatient and c_2 is consumption in period 2 if the individual turns out to be patient.

The expected utility of a representative individual with CRRA preferences and no time discount rate is therefore[3]

$$U = \rho \frac{c_1^{1-\theta}}{1-\theta} + (1-\rho) \frac{c_2^{1-\theta}}{1-\theta} \qquad (7.1)$$

Note that a patient individual who invests all her initial endowment e as well as the maximum amount she can borrow on the international market f in the risk-free project will consume $eR + f(R - 1)$ in period 2. Clearly, only individuals who know that they are impatient will choose to invest in the world market rather than in the domestic project (since this will give them $c_1 = e$ instead of $c_1 = e(1 - r)$).

7.2 Banks

Since individual types are private information, people have an interest in pooling risk and money. Let us therefore assume that they form a bank together where they pool all their resources and that aims to maximize the utility of the representative individual. The individual can withdraw money for consumption either in period 1 or in period 2. The total amount (per depositor) that the bank invests in the investment project is $k > 0$. Furthermore, the bank can borrow money on the international capital market. Let d be the amount of "long-term" borrowing per depositor in period 0 to be repaid in period 2 and b be the equivalent number in period 1 to be repaid in period 2. Since it is beneficial to borrow abroad and invest domestically, it will always be the case that $d + b = f$. The prevalence of impatient individuals who want to consume in period 1 implies that the bank needs to liquidate part of the investment project at this time. $l < k$ is the size of this liquidation.

The timing of events in the model is the following:

- At $t = 0$: Individuals deposit e in the bank and the bank borrows d on the international market. The bank invests this money into a long-run project such that $d + e = k$.
- At $t = 1$: In normal times, a fraction ρ of depositors withdraw c_1 from the bank. In order to cover this withdrawal, the bank borrows an additional amount b on the international market and potentially liquidates part of the project at a loss such that $\rho c_1 = b + rl$. Should a bank run occur, however, all depositors might want to withdraw their money.
- At $t = 2$: The part of the project that has not been liquidated $(k - l)$ yields a return R. This amount needs to be large enough in order for loans $b + d = f$

to be repaid and for patient consumers to withdraw their money: $R(k - l) = (1 - \rho)c_2 + d + b = (1 - \rho)c_2 + f$. A so-called "incentive compatibility constraint" necessary for anyone to want to invest long-term is further that $c_2 \geq c_1$.

What are the socially optimal levels of c_1^*, c_2^*, and l^*, i.e. the solutions that maximize the joint welfare of both patient and impatient individuals? To start with, recall that early liquidation is associated with a loss, which means that $l^* = 0$ must be the socially optimal level.[4] Hence $\rho c_1^* = b$ in period 1, i.e. the bank will satisfy impatient depositors' consumption needs only through international borrowing. In period 2, we will further have that $(1 - \rho)c_2^* + f = Rk$ (recalling that $l^* = 0$).

What we want to do is to rewrite the conditions above into an intertemporal budget constraint. We can manipulate the expressions above,

$$(1 - \rho)c_2^* = Rk - f = R(d + e) - f = R(f - b + e) - f$$
$$= R(f - \rho c_1^* + e) - f$$

and then rearrange the resulting expression so that c_1^* and c_2^* end up on the left-hand side:

$$R\rho c_1^* + (1 - \rho)c_2^* = R(f + e) - f = Re + f(R - 1) \tag{7.2}$$

$$= Rw, \quad \text{where } w = e + \frac{f(R - 1)}{R}$$

The term w thus describes the individual's initial endowment plus the returns to the investment project and might be interpreted as the economy's wealth (per individual). It also serves as the budget constraint for the individual in its utility maximization.

In order to maximize the utility function in (7.1) subject to (7.2), we set up the Lagrangian

$$\Gamma = \rho\frac{c_1^{1-\theta}}{1 - \theta} + (1 - \rho)\frac{c_2^{1-\theta}}{1 - \theta} + \lambda[Rw - R\rho c_1^* - (1 - \rho)c_2^*]$$

where λ is the Lagrange multiplier, as always. The first-order conditions are

$$\frac{\partial\Gamma}{\partial c_1} = \rho c_1^{-\theta} - \lambda R\rho = 0 \tag{7.3}$$

$$\frac{\partial\Gamma}{\partial c_2} = (1 - \rho)c_2^{-\theta} - \lambda(1 - \rho) = 0 \tag{7.4}$$

The solution to this maximization problem can be found by using the following procedure. First, by combining (7.3) and (7.4), it can be shown that the equilibrium levels of consumption are given by $c_2^*/c_1^* = R^{1/\theta}$. Inserting the value for c_1^*

into the budget constraint in (7.2) eventually allows us to express the closed-form equilibrium levels:[5]

$$\rho c_1^* = \alpha w, \quad (1-\rho)c_2^* = wR(1-\alpha) \tag{7.5}$$

$$\text{where } \alpha = \left(1 + \frac{1-\rho}{\rho R^{(\theta-1)/\theta}}\right)^{-1} < 1$$

Not surprisingly, consumption levels in both periods will depend on wealth w. Wealth, in turn, increases linearly with initial endowments e and with the international credit limit f, as we know from (7.2).

The key thing to remember from these solutions so far is that the socially optimal situation is that no premature liquidation occurs, i.e. that $l^* = 0$, but this might still be the actual outcome if too many investors withdraw their money in the first period. We will analyze this aspect more closely next.

7.3 A bank run equilibrium

Let us imagine that banks have the following contract with their depositors. In period 0, depositors surrender to the bank their initial endowment e and their ability to borrow abroad b and d. In return, each individual can withdraw either c_1^* units for consumption in period 1 or c_2^* units in period 2. Note that we will analyze scenarios when even patient individuals for some reason choose to withdraw money in period 1 and thus potentially cause a dangerous bank run. In this case, banks will need to liquidate part of the project ($l > 0$), although this is not socially optimal.

Banks are assumed to face a hard budget constraint in the sense that they must repay their foreign debt in all circumstances. What this means is that the investment project must at least provide enough returns in period 2 to cover period 0 and period 1 loans: $R(k - l) = b + d = f$. Rewriting this condition, and making use of the solutions above, gives us an expression for the maximum level of liquidation that the bank can undertake in the first period:

$$l^+ = \frac{Rk - f}{R} = \frac{(1-\rho)c_2^*}{R} = w(1-\alpha) \tag{7.6}$$

Imagine now that all depositors come and want to withdraw money in the first period, perhaps due to a bank panic. The bank pays out c_1^* to each of them, in accordance with the contract. How long can the bank make such payments?

The answer is that withdrawals (per individual) can be made up to the bank's total liquidation value $b + rl^+$. This is simply the maximum amount of cash assets that the bank can provide in the short term. Should consumption withdrawals exceed short-term foreign loans b plus the highest attainable (premature) project liquidation value rl^+, the bank becomes insolvent and must close down. The foreign loans are then paid back already in period 1, impatient and some patient individuals get their money back, but a number of patient individuals run the risk of losing their savings.

More specifically, if all individuals withdraw their money in period 1, the amount (per individual) will be c_1^*. A *bank run equilibrium* is said to exist if

$$z^+ = c_1^* - (b + rl^+) > 0 \tag{7.7}$$

If this situation prevails, banks cannot survive a sudden withdrawal of all individual savings. z^+ might therefore be referred to as a measure of the bank's illiquidity.

If we insert the equilibrium values derived above into (7.7), we find that

$$z^+ > 0 \quad \text{if } c_1^* - (b + rl^+) = \frac{\alpha w}{\rho} - [\alpha w + rw(1 - \alpha)] > 0$$

It is clear that wealth w is just a scalar in this expression and will not matter for determining the sign. Removing w and recalling that α is given by (7.5) enables us to show that

$$z^+ > 0 \quad \text{if } R^{(\theta-1)/\theta} > r \tag{7.8}$$

Clearly, if $\theta \geq 1$, then a bank run equilibrium will exist, since $R > r$. In the often assumed range of $\theta \in (0, 1)$, (7.8) will not be satisfied and there will not exist a bank run equilibrium. In other words, the more risk-averse individuals are, the more likely that a bank run equilibrium will exist. Whether the equilibrium actually materializes or not depends on individual strategies and on the particular nature of the strategic interaction between individuals. The analysis above describes the fundamental characteristics of the economy that need to be in place for a bank run to be possible.

7.4   Foreign credit

In the scenario above, foreign credit in period 1 (b) was available even if a bank run occurred. What if this was not possible? We know, for instance, that an important feature of the financial crisis of 2008 and onwards was that banks in general were unwilling to lend to each other in the midst of the crisis.

In the model, a failure to receive foreign credit in case of a depositor panic in period 1 would imply that $R(k - l) = d = f$, which in turn would imply that the maximum level of first-period liquidation is

$$l^a = \frac{Rk - d}{R} \tag{7.9}$$

Since $d < f$, it will be the case that $l^a > l^+$ (see (7.6)). The bank's level of illiquidity is

$$z^a = c_1^* - rl^a = c_1^* - r\left(k - \frac{d}{R}\right) \tag{7.10}$$

$$= c_1^* + rd\left(\frac{1}{R} - 1\right) - re$$

By comparing this level with that in (7.7) and using (7.6) and (7.9), we can deduce that

$$z^a - z^+ = b + r(l^+ - l^a) = b\left(1 - \frac{r}{R}\right) > 0$$

In other words, if foreign creditors will not provide loans in period 1 in case of a panic, the bank has a higher illiquidity and is more vulnerable than otherwise, despite the fact that the maximum level of liquidation is higher. This is of course well in line with intuition.

It is even possible that an international refusal to lend might cause a bank run. If the international creditors announce in period 1 that b is not available to the bank, contrary to expectations, depositors will realize that the bank's vulnerability has increased and will therefore try to withdraw as much as possible in period 1, potentially causing the bank to collapse. In this sense, it does not matter if b becomes unavailable through domestic conditions or due to a crisis abroad. It also shows how foreign financial crises can have serious repercussions on the domestic financial sector.

7.5 Short-term debt

In the sections above, even if foreign creditors potentially did not lend during a bank run in period 1, they would still accept having their period 0 loan d repaid in period 2 when the bank's investment project had run its course. But what if creditors demanded all loans to be repaid and the project to be liquidated already in period 1 in the event of a run?

In this case, the bank would have to pay its short-term obligations $c_1^* + d$ by using the liquidation value of the whole project rk:

$$z^b = c_1^* + d - rk = c_1^* + d - r(d + e) = c_1^* + d(1 - r) - re \tag{7.11}$$

Using the same procedure as before and comparing z^a and z^b, we can easily see that $z^b > z^a$, implying that this type of short-term debt rearrangement increases the risk of a bank run even further.

7.6   Liberalizing international credit markets

It seems to be an important policy issue to analyze what happens when international credit markets are liberalized in the sense that f, the international borrowing constraint, is loosened so that f rises. Several empirical studies on financial crises seem to suggest that such major economic upheavals are usually preceded by financial liberalization.

To start with, we know from (7.2) that the economy's wealth increases with an increase in f since foreign credit has a zero interest rate and can earn a return $R > 1$ for every dollar invested. From (7.5), we also see that consumption in both periods will increase. In this sense, a deregulation of the international financial market would increase social welfare.

However, if we assume that the bank lives in a world of short-term debt where $b = 0$ and $d = f$, as just described, we can rewrite (7.11) as

$$z^b = c_1^* + f - rk = \frac{\alpha w}{\rho} + f - r(f + e)$$

$$= \frac{\alpha w}{\rho} + (f - \alpha w)(1 - r) - re$$

$$= \frac{\alpha}{\rho}\left(e + \frac{f(R-1)}{R}\right) + \left[f\left(1 - \alpha + \frac{1}{R}\right) - \alpha e\right](1 - r) - re$$

where we have substituted in the expression for w to the right on the second line.

What comes out very clearly from this equation is that z^b increases with f. In other words, if debts can be easily canceled in the case of a bank run, an increase in capital inflows will increase financial fragility and increase the bank's illiquidity.[6] In this sense, a liberalization of international financial markets is rational ex ante because it increases the socially optimal level of consumption, but is typically regarded as irrational after a financial crisis since increased capital inflows make banks more vulnerable to bank runs.

8 Consumption and Saving

In this chapter, we analyze in depth the determinants of the largest component on the user side of the GDP equation: *aggregate private consumption* C_t. Consumption theory has been a key topic in macroeconomics since the Keynesian revolution in the 1930s. It is also one of the areas where differences between the Keynesian paradigm and the rational expectations paradigm of Milton Friedman and Robert Lucas are most evident.

We start this chapter by briefly reviewing the Keynesian consumption function. We then present an extensive discussion of the permanent income hypothesis where a representative agent maximizes consumption in a multi-period framework. Given the centrality of this model in modern macroeconomics, we give this framework a great deal of attention. We also discuss its offshoot, the random walk model. We then briefly discuss precautionary saving, as well as how the model changes when we introduce time discount rates and interest rates. Sections 8.8 and 8.9 discuss two currently very intensive fields of research: the importance of *relative consumption* concerns and *time inconsistency*.

8.1 The Keynesian consumption function

The standard aggregate consumption function in the Keynesian framework relates current consumption C_t to current disposable income Y_t^d:

$$C_t = c_a + c_{\mathrm{mpc}} Y_t^d = c_a + c_{\mathrm{mpc}}(1 - \tau)Y_t \tag{8.1}$$

In this well-known expression, $c_a > 0$ is the *autonomous* level of consumption that is independent of income, $c_{\mathrm{mpc}} \in (0, 1)$ is the *marginal propensity to consume*, τ is the income tax rate, and Y_t is aggregate current household income. The after-tax net income is thus $Y_t^d = (1 - \tau)Y_t$.

The straightforward implication of this model is that a marginal increase in Y_t will increase consumption by $c_{\mathrm{mpc}}(1 - \tau) > 0$. Also, it is noteworthy that government policy has a strong and immediate effect. A marginal decrease in the income tax rate will increase aggregate consumption by $c_{\mathrm{mpc}} Y_t > 0$.[1] In the Keynesian world, agents are not forward-looking and only react to changes in current income.

8.2   Friedman's critique

In a famous book, Milton Friedman (1957) challenged the Keynesian view by arguing that agents in the real world most likely were able to distinguish between a permanent and a transitory component in the flow of disposable incomes. If current disposable income is Y_t^d, then each individual distinguishes between the long-run average income, or *permanent income*, Y_t^P, and transitory income Y_t^T, where transitory incomes are positive or negative and where the expected level is zero: $E_t(Y_t^T) = E_t(Y_{t+1}^T) = 0$. E_t is an expectations operator showing expectations at time t. Hence, current disposable income equals

$$Y_t^d = Y_t^P + Y_t^T$$

The key new assumption in the *permanent income hypothesis* (PIH) is that decisions regarding current consumption are only based on permanent income rather than on the current income:

$$C_t = Y_t^P \qquad (8.2)$$

The wider implications of this model will be explored in greater detail in the next section, where a more complete version of the model is presented.

8.3   The permanent income hypothesis

As in the OLG model, the standard version of the PIH employs a micro-founded framework with a utility-maximizing representative individual who maximizes lifetime utility, subject to a lifetime budget constraint. Utility is gained solely from the individual's own consumption.[2]

The utility function is

$$U = \sum_{t=0}^{T} \beta^t u(c_t) = u(c_0) + \beta u(c_1) + \beta^2 u(c_2) + \cdots + \beta^T u(c_T) \qquad (8.3)$$

where c_t is individual consumption and where the function has the standard properties $u'(c_t) > 0$ and $u''(c_t) < 0$. There is thus always a positive marginal utility of consumption, but marginal utility is declining as consumption increases. The individual is now assumed to live for $T + 1 > 0$ years.[3] $u(c_t)$ is referred to as the *instantaneous utility function* and is stable over time. $\beta \leq 1$ is a time discount factor, as before.

We assume for simplicity that the individual has a known stream of exogenously future incomes $y_0, y_1, y_2, \ldots, y_T$ and that income tax rates are zero. The lifetime budget constraint (or *permanent income*) is

$$\sum_{t=0}^{T} \frac{c_t}{(1+r)^t} = \sum_{t=0}^{T} \frac{y_t}{(1+r)^t} \qquad (8.4)$$

where $r \geq 0$ is a time-invariant interest rate. There is further a perfect credit market so that individuals can borrow money if $y_t < c_t$, as long as the lifetime budget constraint in (8.4) is satisfied.

Although this intertemporal constraint is really just an extension of the two-period constraint from the OLG model in (5.3), it is worth elaborating a little exactly how (8.4) arises. Consider, for example, a case where $T = 2$. In this case, consumption in the last period must be

$$c_2 = y_2 + (y_1 - c_1)(1+r) + (y_0 - c_0)(1+r)^2$$

That is, the indidual will consume all net savings from previous periods $(y_1 - c_1)(1+r) + (y_0 - c_0)(1+r)^2$ plus last period income y_2. If we isolate the consumption terms on the left-hand side, we can write

$$c_2 + c_1(1+r) + c_0(1+r)^2 = \sum_{t=0}^{2} c_t(1+r)^t$$

$$= y_2 + y_1(1+r) + y_0(1+r)^2 = \sum_{t=0}^{2} y_t(1+r)^t$$

Normally, we want to rewrite the budget constraint so that it expresses the present value in period 0, i.e. when the decision about the consumption plan is made. By dividing both sides by $(1+r)^2$, we end up with the expression in (8.4) when $T = 2$, which shows that the present value of lifetime consumption must be equal to the present value of lifetime incomes.

8.3.1 Utility maximization over the life cycle

The utility function in (8.3) and the budget constraint in (8.4) together form a maximization problem for the individual where the challenge is to find the levels of affordable consumption that maximize utility. We therefore set up a Lagrangian function

$$\Gamma = \sum_{t=0}^{T} \beta^t u(c_t) + \lambda \left(\sum_{t=0}^{T} \frac{c_t}{(1+r)^t} - \sum_{t=0}^{T} \frac{y_t}{(1+r)^t} \right) \tag{8.5}$$

where $\lambda > 0$ is a standard Lagrange multiplier. Note that the choice variables for this optimization are the levels of consumption for each time period: c_0, c_1, c_2, etc.

The first-order conditions for a maximum are thus

$$\frac{\partial \Gamma}{\partial c_0} = u'(c_0) - \lambda = 0 \tag{8.6}$$

$$\frac{\partial \Gamma}{\partial c_1} = \beta u'(c_1) - \frac{\lambda}{1+r} = 0$$

$$\cdots$$

$$\frac{\partial \Gamma}{\partial c_T} = \beta^T u'(c_T) - \frac{\lambda}{(1+r)^T} = 0$$

These first-order conditions imply that $u'(c_0^*) = \lambda = \beta(1+r)u'(c_1^*) = \beta^2(1+r)^2 u'(c_2^*) \cdots = \beta^T(1+r)^T u'(c_T^*)$. Hence, we once again obtain the familiar Euler equation, already derived in the OLG model, but now in a $(T+1)$-period framework:

$$\frac{u'(c_t^*)}{u'(c_{t+1}^*)} = \beta(1+r) \quad \text{for all } t \in \{0, 1, 2, \ldots, T-1\}$$

8.4   An example

In order to develop the intuition for the PIH result further, let us make the highly simplifying assumption that $\beta = 1$ and that $r = 0$. In that case, the Euler equation reduces to $u'(c_0^*) = \lambda = u'(c_1^*) = \cdots = u'(c_T^*)$. In other words, optimally, the marginal utility of consumption should be the same in all periods. Since $u(c_t)$ is strictly concave, there can only be one unique level of c_t where marginal utility (the slope of the utility function) is $u'(c_t) = \lambda$. Hence, the individual will optimally set a level of consumption such that $c_t^* = c_{t+1}^* = c_{t+2}^* = \cdots = c_T^*$. This result of identical optimal levels of consumption throughout life is sometimes referred to as *consumption smoothing*.

The fact that the optimal level of consumption is identical throughout an individual's lifetime T means that we can reformulate the budget constraint as

$$\sum_{t=0}^{T} c_t = (T+1)c_t^* = \sum_{t=0}^{T} y_t$$

Dividing both sides by life length $T+1$ gives us the key expression for consumption in the PIH:

$$c_t^* = \frac{\sum_{t=0}^{T} y_t}{T+1} \tag{8.7}$$

The interpretation of this expression is simply that an individual will optimally consume in every period her average annual income. Clearly, the optimal level of consumption will increase if income level y_t increases. What is the impact of an increase in T? That will of course depend on the intertemporal structure of the income flow. If it is the case that all individuals retire at some $t^r < T$ whereafter $Y_t = 0$, then an increase in T (i.e. a longer life) will imply a lower level of consumption today since the flow of incomes must last longer.

8.4.1 Saving

In the PIH, savings (positive or negative) are used to smooth the time pattern of consumption. Current income is $y_t = c_t + s_t$. Hence, the expression for optimal saving in the PIH is

$$s_t^* = y_t - c_t^* = y_t - \frac{\sum_{t=0}^{T} y_t}{T+1} \tag{8.8}$$

where s_t^* is positive if current incomes are relatively large and negative if current income in period t is lower than the optimal level of consumption.[4]

An important implication of the expression (8.8) is that whereas the level of consumption is constant over time and is insensitive to the time distribution of incomes $y_1, y_2, \ldots, y_T$, savings are very sensitive to current incomes. To be more precise, the derivative of s_t^* with respect to y_t is $1 - 1/(T+1) > 0$ whereas the derivative of c_t^* with respect to y_t is only $1/(T+1)$. The sensitivity of savings with respect to current incomes is larger if T is large. A prediction from these results would thus be that savings should display a greater degree of variation over life than consumption levels.

8.4.2 Mid-term analysis

If we only observe an individual in mid-life, i.e. at some $t = \tau$ such that $0 < \tau < T$, then in order to understand the individual's consumption choice, we must take into account past incomes and savings as well as future incomes. Note that since $(T+1)c_\tau^* = \sum_{t=0}^{T} y_t$, we can write

$$c_\tau^* = \sum_{t=0}^{T} y_t - Tc_\tau^* = \sum_{t=0}^{\tau-1} y_t - \tau c_\tau^* + \sum_{t=\tau}^{T} y_t - (T-\tau)c_\tau^* \tag{8.9}$$

$$= A_{\tau-1} + \sum_{t=\tau}^{T} y_t - (T-\tau)c_\tau^*$$

In this expression, $\sum_{t=0}^{\tau-1} y_t - \tau c_\tau^* = A_{\tau-1}$ shows accumulated incomes minus total consumption spendings from $t = 0$ to $\tau - 1$. If $A_{\tau-1} > 0$, the individual has positive assets at the time of analysis τ, and negative if $A_{\tau-1} < 0$.

If we isolate c_τ^* on the left-hand side and then divide both sides by $T + 1 - \tau$, we obtain

$$c_\tau^* = \frac{A_{\tau-1} + \sum_{t=\tau}^{T} y_t}{T + 1 - \tau}$$

A commonly shown version of this expression is when it is assumed that $\tau = 1$. The expression then collapses into the very simple form

$$c_1^* = \frac{A_0 + \sum_{t=1}^{T} y_t}{T} \tag{8.10}$$

Note that, in this case, $A_0 = y_0 - c_0^*$, so that it shows accumulated savings from previous periods. The net level of assets A_0 can be positive or negative, depending on the individual's incomes during young age.

In some of the expositions below, we will work with versions of an intertemporal maximization problem that builds on the logic of expression (8.10).

8.4.3   Life-cycle implications

In the real world, there is of course never perfect information about future incomes. According to the life-cycle hypothesis of consumption, however, we can make the following reasonable projection about the time distribution of current incomes. In the first phase of an individual's life (let us call it period 0), education and human capital will be acquired and incomes will typically be low. In this phase, individuals are net borrowers with negative savings. In "middle age" (period 1), people will work and usually be able to accumulate substantial savings.[5] In the third phase (period 2), finally, people retire from work and live mainly off the savings accumulated during working years.[6] Consumption should, according to theory, remain at a fairly constant level throughout the three periods.

To illustrate this insight, let us assume that the flow of incomes from young to old age is y_0, y_1, and y_2 and that $y_0 < y_2 < y_1$ as in Figure 8.1. Incomes are thus lowest when people are young and highest when people are middle-aged. Lifetime incomes are $\sum_{t=0}^{2} y_t$ and a consumption smoothing individual should choose to consume $c_t^* = \sum_{t=0}^{2} y_t / 3$. Hence, we know for sure that $y_0 < c_t^* < y_1$, i.e. that young people will tend to consume above their earnings, whereas the reverse is true for most people of middle age. In the scenario described here, we cannot predict anything definite about consumption relative to income during old age. In the example in Figure 8.1, $y_2 < c_t^*$.

8.4.4   Policy implications

Comparing the result in (8.7) with the typical Keynesian aggregate consumption function $C_t = c_a + c_{mpc} Y_t$, a number of very different policy implications will emerge. A temporary increase in income ΔY_t, perhaps due to a temporary government subsidy, should increase consumption by $c_{mpc} \Delta Y_t$. If we, for instance,

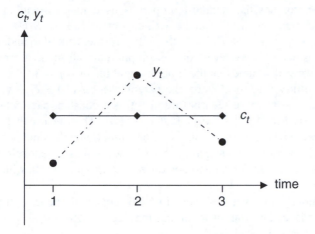

Figure 8.1 Example of consumption and income over the life cycle.

assume $c_{\text{mpc}} = 1/2$ and $\Delta Y_t = 10$, then $\Delta C_t \approx 5$. However, in the PIH scenario, an identical increase in income should increase consumption only by $\Delta Y_t / T$. If we assume a middle-aged person in the Western world at 40 years who can expect to live for another 40 years, the increase in consumption will be only $10/40 = 0.4$.[7]

The more far-reaching implication of this example is that short-run policy efforts aimed at boosting consumption are likely to be fairly successful if we assume a Keynesian consumption function, but they will be very ineffective in the PIH framework.

8.5 The random-walk model

A major weakness of the simple version of the PIH shown above was that individuals could make perfect assessments of their lifetime incomes. An important feature of real-world economic decisions is that there is always a substantial degree of uncertainty about the future and that we can only make informed guesses about our future economic situation. In Hall's (1978) *random-walk model*, which is an extension of the PIH framework, a key feature is that individuals form expectations about uncertain future incomes and that these expectations are continually updated. Individuals are forward-looking and take into account all available information at some time t. In economics terminology, we refer to assessments of this kind as *rational expectations*.[8]

An individual's expected utility at some (mid-life) year $t = 1$ is now quadratic:

$$E_1(U) = E_1 \sum_{t=1}^{T} \left(c_t - \frac{a}{2} c_t^2 \right) \tag{8.11}$$

E_t is an expectations operator indicating that expectations are made at time t. The expectations operator has the standard properties used in statistical theory.[9] Note that the expression (8.11) can be written out in full as $E_1(U) = E_1(c_1 - \frac{a}{2}c_1^2) + E_1(c_2 - \frac{a}{2}c_2^2) + \cdots + E_1(c_T - \frac{a}{2}c_T^2)$. It is further central to understand that expectations about future levels of consumption are all made at time $t = 1$. For simplicity, we still assume that the time discount factor is $\beta = 1$.

The instantaneous utility function (inside the parentheses) $u_t(c_t) = c_t - \frac{a}{2}c_t^2$ is also different from what we have seen before. $a > 0$ is a constant parameter. Marginal utility of c_t is $u_t'(c_t) = 1 - ac_t > 0$ if $c_t < 1/a$. This means that if consumption levels exceed $1/a$, marginal utility of consumption will actually be negative. Although this might be an interesting scenario, we will assume levels of consumption such that $c_t < 1/a$. The second derivative is $u_t''(c_t) = -a < 0$, which ensures concavity.

The budget constraint is equivalent to the one implied above with the exception that we have now introduced uncertainty about lifetime incomes. $A_0 = y_0 - c_0^*$ has the same interpretation as above and $r = 0$:

$$\sum_{t=1}^{T} E_1(c_t) \leq A_0 + \sum_{t=1}^{T} E_1(y_t) \tag{8.12}$$

By setting up the Lagrangian Γ as in (8.5) and taking first-order conditions for a maximum $\frac{\partial \Gamma}{\partial c_t} = E_1(1 - ac_t) - \lambda = 0$ for all $t = 1, 2, \ldots, T$, we obtain the familiar Euler equation: $1 - ac_1 = E_1(1 - ac_2) = \cdots = E_1(1 - ac_T)$. Note that the expectations operator is absent from the first term since c_1 is observed at time 1. The general result is hence that $1 - ac_1 = 1 - aE_1(c_t)$, where $t > 1$. By canceling 1 and a from this expression, we get the optimal consumption path:

$$c_1^* = E_1(c_t^*) \tag{8.13}$$

In other words, at the time of decision, the individual expects to consume the same amount at all future dates as he or she currently consumes.

Inserting this result into the budget constraint yields the key result of the random-walk model:

$$c_1^* = \frac{1}{T}\left(A_0 + \sum_{t=1}^{T} E_1(y_t)\right) \tag{8.14}$$

This expression is identical to the one in (8.10) except for the expectations operator E_1. The interpretation is also similar to the one above: the individual consumes every period a fraction $1/T$ of his or her expected lifetime resources. A noteworthy feature is that the presence of uncertainty does not really seem to affect the individual's consumption choice. The individual values $\sum_{t=1}^{T} E_1(y_t)$ as equivalent to $\sum_{t=1}^{T} y_t$ in (8.7). Hall's random-walk model is therefore sometimes described as being characterized by *certainty equivalence*. We will relax this assumption below.

8.5.1 *Introducing a stochastic component*

In order to describe how uncertainty can enter the model, let us imagine that actual consumption at some date t is given by

$$c_t = E_{t-1}(c_t^*) + e_t = c_{t-1}^* + e_t \qquad (8.15)$$

In this simple expression, e_t is a stochastic error term with the property that $E_{t-1}(e_t) = 0$. e_t reflects that there is an element of uncertainty since actual consumption might turn out to be higher ($e_t > 0$) or lower ($e_t < 0$) that what was expected at $t - 1$. Furthermore, we know from (8.13) that $E_{t-1}(c_t^*) = c_{t-1}^*$. Hence, the prediction is that consumption at t equals consumption at $t - 1$, plus a random component that is realized at t.

In the language of time series econometrics, the process in (8.15) is one characterized by a *random walk*. This implies that the time pattern of consumption is without any trend and that it does not fluctuate around any mean.[10]

It is also important to emphasize that at each time period t, individuals use all available information about the future in forming their consumption decision (see (8.14)). Indeed, if they did not, they would not have rational expectations. Each c_t^* is thus a reflection of all available information about future incomes and other relevant facts, and since individuals have a preference for consumption smoothing, they have reason to believe that they will consume c_t^* throughout their future lives.

How should we then think about the random component e_t? By the logic of rational expectations, it must be the case that e_t arises due to some new information about our future prospects that was not available at $t - 1$. Random events that change our view on our future economic situation indeed happen all the time and, for instance, include serious injury by accident, unexpected new job opportunities, or lottery prizes. More formally, if we want to study changes in consumption between periods 1 and 2 in the framework above so that $c_2 = c_1^* + e_2$, then the error term is given by

$$e_2 = \frac{1}{T-1}\left(\sum_{t=2}^{T} E_2(y_t) - \sum_{t=2}^{T} E_1(y_t)\right) \qquad (8.16)$$

In other words, if the error term is different from zero, expectations about the flow of incomes over the discrete interval from $t = 2$ to $t = T$ must have changed from period 1 to period 2.[11] Whether aggregate consumption actually follows a random walk as proposed by Hall (1978) has been a source of numerous empirical studies in macroeconomics.

8.6 Precautionary saving

A weakness with the models above is that there is no real motivation to "save for a rainy day". Even in the presence of uncertainty, as in Hall's framework, individuals behave as if the flow of future incomes was certain (which is referred to as *certainty equivalence* above). Below we introduce an extension of the model that helps us explain the prevalence of *precautionary saving*.

From a theoretical point of view, we know from the Euler equation above that the condition for optimality is

$$u'(c_t) = E_t u'(c_{t+1}) \Longrightarrow$$
$$1 - ac_t = E_t(1 - ac_{t+1}) \Longrightarrow 1 - aE_t(c_{t+1}) = u'[E_t(c_{t+1})]$$

A key technical aspect of this expression is that the expected marginal utility of c_{t+1} equals the marginal utility of the expected value of c_{t+1}: $E_t u'(c_{t+1}) = u'[E_t(c_{t+1})]$. This is a feature that follows from the quadratic utility function in the random-walk model, and the exact meaning of this will be demonstrated below.

One problem with the quadratic utility function is, as mentioned above, that it allows for a situation where $u'(c_t) < 0$ at $c_t > 1/a$. A negative marginal utility of consumption at high levels of consumption is problematic in terms of realism. Note also that in the quadratic case, $u'''(c_t) = 0$. If, however, we assumed $u'''(c_t) > 0$, marginal utility would be a negative and convex function of consumption, as illustrated in Figure 8.2.

If the only new assumption is that $u'''(c_t) > 0$ at all $c_t > 0$, then $E_t u'(c_{t+1})$ must be higher than before (due to the convexity of $u'(c_t)$). At the old level of c_t, we then have that $u'[E_t(c_{t+1})] < E_t u'(c_{t+1})$, i.e. a violation of the Euler condition. In order to restore the equilibrium in the Euler equation, there must be an increase in $u'[E_t(c_{t+1})] = u'(c_t)$. This can only come about through a decrease in c_t. A reduction in consumption at time t means an equivalent increase in that period's savings. Hence, the new assumption that $u'''(c_t) > 0$ leads to precautionary saving.

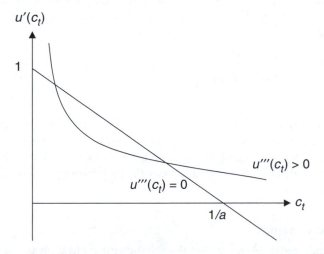

Figure 8.2 Precautionary saving and the third derivative of the utility function.

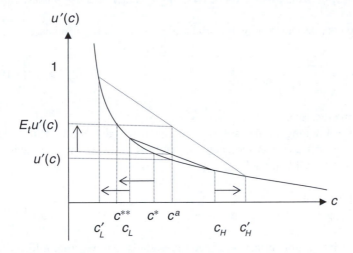

Figure 8.3 Precautionary saving with an increase in uncertainty.

A more intuitive explanation is given in Figure 8.3. There we assume that consumption can assume either a high value c_H with a probability of 1/2 or a low value c_L with a probability of 1/2. Hence, the expected level of consumption is $E_t(c) = c^a = (c_H + c_L)/2$. However, at c^a, we have $u'(c^a) < E_t u'(c) = [u'(c_H) + u'(c_L)]/2$. Only at c^* will we have that $u'(c^*) = E_t u'(c^*)$, which will therefore be the chosen, lower level of consumption.

If uncertainty increases in the sense that c_L decreases (to c_L') by exactly the same amount as c_H increases (to c_H'), then the expected value c^a is preserved. However, the change in risk causes a drastic increase in $E_t u'(c)$. This is indeed a direct consequence of the assumption of $u'''(c_t) > 0$. In order to restore the Euler equation, c must now decrease even further to $c^{**} < c^*$. Hence, the increase in risk decreases the optimal level of consumption and increases savings. This is the key insight from models of precautionary saving.

8.7 Interest rates and time discount rates

Let us now reintroduce interest rates and time discount rates into the model and analyze the implications.

From the OLG model, we borrow the CRRA utility function with a finite time horizon of T:

$$U = \sum_{t=0}^{T} \frac{1}{(1+\rho)^t} \frac{c_t^{1-\theta}}{1-\theta} \tag{8.17}$$

As before, $\theta \in (0, 1)$ is the relative risk-aversion parameter and $\rho \geq 0$ is the time discount rate.

The individual's intertemporal budget constraint in the multi-period case is

$$\sum_{t=0}^{T} \frac{c_t}{(1+r)^t} = \sum_{t=0}^{T} \frac{y_t}{(1+r)^t} \tag{8.18}$$

where r is the interest rate.

Setting up the Lagrangian and solving for the first-order conditions in the standard way, we will arrive at the same "discrete Ramsey result" for relative consumption as in the OLG model:

$$c_t^* = c_0^* \left(\frac{1+r}{1+\rho} \right)^{\frac{t}{\theta}} \tag{8.19}$$

One of the more interesting aspects of this expression is that we are not likely to have consumption smoothing any more. If, for instance, $r > \rho$ (which should be the case in dynamic, thrifty societies), then consumption will increase exponentially over time and will *not* display a random walk.[12] Figure 8.4 shows examples of the optimal consumption paths for three different scenarios: $r > \rho$, $r = \rho$, and $r < \rho$. As before, the optimal growth rate of consumption is given by

$$\frac{c_{t+1}^* - c_t^*}{c_t^*} = g_c^* = \left(\frac{1+r}{1+\rho} \right)^{\frac{1}{\theta}} - 1$$

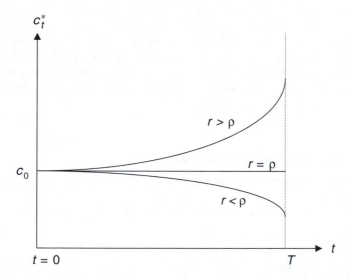

Figure 8.4 Optimal consumption paths over time for different levels of r and ρ.

8.8 Relative consumption

Recent research, inspired by experimental studies, has demonstrated that the individual's utility is determined not only by her own absolute level of consumption but also by her relative level, compared with some reference point R. The reference point might, for instance, be the neighbor's level of consumption – in which case the individual will have so-called "keeping up with the Joneses" concerns – or it could be derived from past levels of her own consumption, in which case "habit formation" plays a role in utility.[13]

As a simple illustration of these ideas, consider the following utility function for two periods with properties similar to that in Bowman et al (1999):

$$U = u(c_1) + v(c_1 - R_1) + u(c_2) + v(c_2 - R_2) \tag{8.20}$$

The function $u(c_t)$ is an instantaneous function of absolute consumption levels as before, with the standard properties of $u'(c_t) > 0$ and $u''(c_t) < 0$. The $v(x)$ function (sometimes referred to as the *gain–loss function*), where $x = c_t - R_t$, introduces reference dependence into the model. $v(x)$ is assumed to have the following properties:

- $v'(x) > 0$ at all x;
- $v(0) = 0$;
- $v''(x) < 0$ for all $x > 0$, and $v''(x) > 0$ for all $x < 0$.

The first assumption means that the individual will always be better off the greater her own level of consumption is compared to the reference point R_t. The second assumption simply means that if consumption is at the reference point, utility from that period will be equal to $u(c_t)$. The third assumption is more far-reaching and implies that the individual has *loss aversion*. This means that her gain–loss function is concave above the reference point and convex below. The deeper meaning is that individuals are even more sensitive to losses than in the standard concave utility setting, which is what defines loss aversion.

The reference point might further be endogenous to the decisions made in the model. It is common to assume an exogenous reference point in the first period R_1. R_2 might, however, depend on c_1:

$$R_2 = (1 - \alpha)R_1 + \alpha c_1 \tag{8.21}$$

An $\alpha = 0$ simply means that the reference point is constant in the two periods. If $\alpha > 0$, however, R_2 is influenced by c_1. If $c_1 > R_1$, then $R_2 > R_1$ and the individual is subject to habit formation.

A key implication of the prevalence of habit formation is that the intertemporal consumption choice is no longer time-independent, as in the PIH.[14] The individual's consumption decision for period 1 will affect utility in period 2 since a very high level of consumption in period 1 will make the individual "addicted" to a high level of consumption, which will affect how she values c_2.

In the case where $\alpha = 0$, so that the reference point is some exogenous factor, it is usually assumed that the individual will compare her own consumption with that of some other person, perhaps the average consumption level in the country or the consumption of neighbors or friends. The exact implications of such relative consumption comparisons depend on the characteristics of the $u(c_t)$ and $v(t)$ functions. Research on the impact of reference-dependent utility is currently very intensive, and it remains to be seen how it will change macroeconomic models of aggregate consumption.

8.9 Time inconsistency

Another frequently demonstrated anomaly in consumer behavior is that people appear to have time-inconsistent preferences in the sense that there is a utility bias towards present consumption that goes beyond normal time discounting. The model analyzed here follows Laibson (1997), while a general overview is provided by Frederick et al (2002).

Let us assume as above that we have a standard concave utility function $u(c_t)$ such that $u'(c_t) > 0$ and $u''(c_t) < 0$, and a standard time discount factor $\beta \leq 1$. Let us, however, make the new assumption that there is a bias towards current consumption in the utility function such that all future time periods are discounted by an additional factor $\gamma \in (0, 1)$. In that case, the lifetime utility of an individual is

$$U = u(c_0) + \gamma\beta u(c_2) + \gamma\beta^2 u(c_3) + \cdots \qquad (8.22)$$

$$= u(c_0) + \gamma \sum_{t=1}^{T} \beta^t u(c_t)$$

The lifetime budget constraint is still given by (8.4). By setting up the Lagrangian in the standard way and rearranging the first-order conditions, we find that the intertemporal marginal rate of substitution between any two periods $t > 0$ is

$$\frac{u'(c_t)}{u'(c_{t+1})} = \beta(1 + r) \qquad (8.23)$$

whereas the same calculation for the the initial period 0 and period 1 gives us

$$\frac{u'(c_0)}{u'(c_1)} = \gamma\beta(1 + r) \qquad (8.24)$$

Note that the only difference from the standard result is the inclusion of $\gamma < 1$. In this sense, preferences are clearly time-inconsistent.

If we also assume the usual CRRA utility such that $u(c_t) = c_t^{1-\theta}/(1-\theta)$, then we get the standard Ramsey result that $c_{t+1}/c_t = [\beta(1+r)]^{\frac{1}{\theta}}$ for all $t > 1$ but that

$$c_0 = \frac{c_1}{[\gamma\beta(1+r)]^{\frac{1}{\theta}}} \tag{8.25}$$

Since $\gamma < 1$, this implies that the individual will consume relatively more in the first period than if $\gamma = 1$, as in the time-consistent, standard case. In each period of the individual's remaining life, there will then be a bias present that will make the individual consume relatively more in the current period. This will not be sustainable, since the lifetime budget constraint is the same as before, and sharp decreases in consumption typically become unavoidable as time approaches T.

9   Investment and Asset Markets

Investments are efforts aimed at increasing a stock of capital, usually physical capital.[1] A country's investments are closely associated with its savings, as shown in the neoclassical growth model. In this chapter, we will present the standard neoclassical model of investment, based on the profit maximization of an individual firm, and derive central results such as *Tobin's marginal q* and the *user cost of capital*. We will also discuss the nature of adjustment costs and how their characteristics affect firms' investment decisions. The account of investment theory outlined here relies on Branson (1989), Caballero (1997), and Romer (2005).

In Section 9.4 we will briefly consider the housing market and analyze the determinants of housing demand and equilibrium price levels.

9.1   The Keynesian investment function

In the simplest Keynesian model, aggregate investment in physical capital is a function of the aggregate level of income Y_t and the interest rate r_t, denoted by $I_t(Y_t, r_t)$, where $\frac{\partial I_t(Y_t, r_t)}{\partial Y_t} > 0$ and $\frac{\partial I_t(Y_t, r_t)}{\partial r_t} < 0$. The prediction that investment should increase with Y follows from an assumption of a long-run relationship between the capital stock K_t and Y_t.[2] Higher interest rates r_t mean that it is more expensive for producers to hold capital, which should decrease investment (just as a higher wage level will induce firms to reduce the number of workers). The Keynesian investment function, however, is not based on any micro foundations of firm behavior. This is what we will turn to next.

9.2   The firm's investment decision

When considering the optimal level of investments, firm owners maximize the present value of future profit streams:

$$V(0) = \sum_{t=0}^{T} \frac{\Pi_t}{(1+r)^t} = \sum_{t=0}^{T} \frac{1}{(1+r)^t}[P_t F(L_t, K_t) - w_t L_t - P_t^I I_t] \qquad (9.1)$$

In this expression, Π_t is total profits in the economy at time t, r is the interest rate, P_t is the price (index) of firms' total produced output $Y_t = F(L_t, K_t)$ (which is a function of labor L_t and physical capital K_t), w_t is the wage rate, P_t^I is the price of the investment good, and I_t is total gross investment. The production function $F(L_t, K_t)$ is characterized by $\frac{\partial F(L_t, K_t)}{\partial L_t} = F_{L_t} > 0$ and $F_{K_t} > 0$. The lifetime of the firm is from 0 to T.

Capital accumulates according to

$$K_{t+1} = K_t + I_t - \delta K_t = K_t(1 - \delta) + I_t \tag{9.2}$$

where I_t is gross investment ($I_t = K_{t+1} - K_t + \delta K_t$, i.e. net investment $K_{t+1} - K_t$ plus replacement investment δK_t) and δ is the rate of capital depreciation.

The firm's maximization problem is

$$\max_{L_t, K_t, I_t} V(0) = \sum_{t=0}^{T} \frac{\Pi_t}{(1+r)^t} \quad \text{s.t. } K_{t+1} = K_t(1 - \delta) + I_t \text{ at each } t = (0, 1, \ldots, T)$$

$$\tag{9.3}$$

This defines a Lagrangian function

$$\Gamma = \sum_{t=0}^{T} \frac{1}{(1+r)^t} [P_t F(L_t, K_t) - w_t L_t - P_t^I I_t] + \sum_{t=0}^{T} \lambda_t [I_t + K_t(1 - \delta) - K_{t+1}]$$

$$\tag{9.4}$$

The relevant first-order conditions for this problem are

$$\frac{\partial \Gamma}{\partial L_t} = \frac{1}{(1+r)^t}(P_t F_{L_t} - w_t) = 0 \tag{9.5}$$

$$\frac{\partial \Gamma}{\partial K_t} = \frac{P_t f_{K_t}}{(1+r)^t} + \lambda_t(1 - \delta) - \lambda_{t-1} = 0 \tag{9.6}$$

$$\frac{\partial \Gamma}{\partial I_t} = -\frac{P_t^I}{(1+r)^t} + \lambda_t = 0 \tag{9.7}$$

Note that the λ_{t-1} in (9.6) comes from the fact that K_t also appears in the restriction for period $t - 1$: $\lambda_{t-1}[I_{t-1} + K_{t-1}(1 - \delta) - K_t]$.

9.2.1 The user cost of capital

From (9.7), we find that

$$\lambda_t = \frac{P_t^I}{(1+r)^t}, \text{ implying that } \lambda_{t-1} = \frac{P_{t-1}^I}{(1+r)^{t-1}}$$

Substituting this result into (9.6) yields

$$\frac{P_t F_{K_t}}{(1+r)^t} + \frac{P_t^I(1-\delta)}{(1+r)^t} - \frac{P_{t-1}^I}{(1+r)^{t-1}} = 0$$

If we first isolate $\frac{P_t F_{K_t}}{(1+r)^t}$ on the left-hand side and then multiply both sides by $(1+r)^t / P_t$, we obtain

$$F_{K_t} = \frac{\delta P_t^I + r P_{t-1}^I - (P_t^I - P_{t-1}^I)}{P_t} = \frac{C_t}{P_t} \tag{9.8}$$

What we have derived is the *real user cost of capital* C_t / P_t. The user cost of capital C_t contains three terms: the *depreciation cost* of investing in capital δP_t^I, plus the *interest cost* of holding capital during t valued at $t-1$, $r P_{t-1}^I$, minus the possible increase in the price of the investment good (which an investor benefits from), $P_t^I - P_{t-1}^I$. The nominal user cost C_t is divided by the price index P_t to yield the real user cost of capital.

The expression in (9.8) implies that firms should optimally make investments up to the level where the marginal product of capital F_{K_t} equals the real user cost C_t / P_t. This equilibrium level is implicitly given in (9.8) such that

$$K_t^* = K(Y_t, C_t, P_t)$$

where $Y_t = F(L_t, K_t)$ is total output in the economy.

9.2.2   A Cobb–Douglas example

In order to obtain a closed-form solution for K^*, let us use the conventional Cobb–Douglas production function

$$Y_t = A K_t^\alpha L_t^{1-\alpha} \tag{9.9}$$

where A is some positive productivity parameter and $0 < \alpha < 1$ is the output elasticity of capital. With this function, we have a marginal product of capital equal to $F_{K_t} = A\alpha K_t^{\alpha-1} L_t^{1-\alpha} = \alpha Y_t / K_t$. Inserting this value back into (9.8), we get

$$\frac{\alpha Y_t}{K_t^*} = \frac{C_t}{P_t}$$

which in turn implies that

$$K_t^* = \frac{\alpha P_t Y_t}{C_t}$$

In other words, the optimal level of capital increases with the price level P_t and with total output Y_t and decreases with the (nominal) user cost C_t.

9.2.3 Tobin's q

The expression for the real user cost of capital might be rearranged into

$$P_t F_{K_t} + P_t^I (1 - \delta) - P_{t-1}^I (1 + r) = 0$$

If we first isolate $P_{t-1}^I (1 + r)$ on the right-hand side and then multiply both sides by $1/[P_{t-1}^I (1 + r)]$, we obtain

$$\frac{1}{1+r} \frac{P_t F_{K_t} + P_t^I (1 - \delta)}{P_{t-1}^I} = 1 \tag{9.10}$$

The term on the left-hand side is referred to as Tobin's marginal q after Nobel Prize laureate James Tobin. It shows the change in the value of the firm at t of a marginal increase in the capital stock at $t - 1$, $P_t F_{K_t} + P_t^I (1 - \delta)$, divided by the cost of acquiring that marginal increase P_{t-1}^I, and discounted back to period $t - 1$, $1/(1+r)$.

The increase in the value of the firm arises from an increase in revenue $P_t F_{K_t}$ and from an increase in the value of its capital $P_t^I (1 - \delta)$. Note that F_{K_t} decreases with K_t due to diminishing returns. In equilibrium, the discounted increased value of the firm should be equal to the cost of a marginal unit of capital P_{t-1}^I. If the firm is not in equilibrium so that Tobin's q is greater (or smaller) than unity, then the marginal benefit of a small increase (decrease) in the capital stock will exceed the marginal cost. Thus the capital stock will be expanded until it reaches the optimal level K^* where Tobin's marginal q is one, as required.

9.3 Adjustment costs

The firm's costs of investment come not only from the purchase of capital. It is usually assumed that the main source of adjustment costs is the demands on internal reorganization of activities. For instance, new computers with new software require both installation and training of workers, which are costs that go beyond the purchase costs.

Let us define adjustment costs as $A(I_t)$ with the property that $A'(I_t) > 0$ so that adjustment costs increase with the size of investment. If such costs are present, the new profit function becomes

$$\sum_{t=0}^{T} \frac{1}{(1+r)^t} [P_t F(L_t, K_t) - w_t L_t - P_t^I I_t - A(I_t)] \tag{9.11}$$

and the new first-order condition for investment is

$$\frac{\partial \Gamma}{\partial I_t} = \frac{-P_t^I - A'(I_t)}{(1+r)^t} + \lambda_t = 0 \tag{9.12}$$

while the other conditions are as before. This further means that

$$\lambda_t = \frac{P_t^I + A'(I_t)}{(1+r)^t} \tag{9.13}$$

The expressions indicate that the introduction of adjustment costs will make the marginal cost of investment higher than before. This in turn implies that investments should generally be smaller than without adjustment costs.

9.3.1   Types of adjustment costs

The literature discusses three major types of adjustment costs. One key source of adjustment costs is *investment irreversibility*. After having purchased a unit of capital, it might have a very low second-hand value. Though increasing a capital stock is easy, it is often much more difficult to decrease a capital stock. One example is a factory, built so that it will exactly fit the production needs of the firm that acquired it. Since it is unlikely that an identical firm exists nearby with identical needs, the factory might be hard to sell should that be necessary.

A simple way to characterize costs of irreversibility is

$$A(I_t) = (P^I - P^S)I_t \tag{9.14}$$

where $P^I - P^S$ is the difference between purchase and the potential sale prices. If this difference is large, the firm will only buy the unit of capital if it is quite sure that it is not going to need to sell it in the near future.

A second type of adjustment costs is one where there is a substantial fixed cost component:

$$A(I_t) = F + \kappa(I_t) \tag{9.15}$$

where $F > 0$ is a fixed cost and where adjustment also has a flexible component $\kappa'(I_t) > 0$. A fixed cost could, for instance, be that a firm must make a large discrete change in how its goods are produced after the investment. Irreversibilities and fixed adjustment costs both imply that investments should appear in a discontinuous (lumpy) fashion, with long periods of inactivity ended by investment "spikes".

A third and quite different kind of adjustment costs are those that are biased towards small, incremental changes:

$$A(I_t) = \frac{aI_t^2}{2} \tag{9.16}$$

In this expression, $a > 0$ is a parameter. We further assume that I_t can be negative if the capital stock is reduced. Taking derivatives, we find that $A'(I_t) = aI > 0$ if $I > 0$ and that $A'(I_t) = aI < 0$ if $I < 0$. Hence, both positive and negative investments (disinvestments) will incur a positive marginal cost. Furthermore, $A''(I_t) = a > 0$, which means that costs are convex. Convexity in turn implies that the costs of changing the capital stock will increase more than proportionally with the size of the change. Hence, in this case, investors will be biased towards incremental changes. The type of adjustment cost that the firm has will of course depend on the structure of production and on the nature of the firm.

9.4 The housing market

The single most important investment decision that a typical household makes over its lifetime is the choice of whether and when to buy a place to live. In making this decision, the household members need to consider their optimal mix of consumption of ordinary goods and the utility provided by owning a house.

If we think of this as a static problem, let us denote the size of the housing stock as H (perhaps reflecting the number of square meters), which is multiplied by p^H (the price per unit of housing) in order to get the total value of the household's housing stock at a given time, $p^H H$.[3] If a house is bought, the household borrows the whole amount. In each period of time, the household has to pay $rp^H H$ in interest. For simplicity, we assume that no repayments need to be made during the period under consideration. In addition to this, the household needs to pay for repair and maintenance an amount $\delta p^H H$, where $\delta > 0$ is the depreciation of the housing stock. The total cost of housing in one period is thus $(r + \delta) p^H H$.

The household earns an income y during each period. This income is used for consumption c and for housing such that

$$c + (r + \delta) p^H H \leq y$$

For simplicity, there are there are no savings.

Let us further assume that the household gets utility from consumption and from living in a house. The utility function is loglinear:

$$U = \ln c + \eta \ln H \tag{9.17}$$

In this function, $\eta > 0$ shows the relative importance given to housing. If $\eta > 1$, then the household gets a higher relative marginal utility from housing than from consumption of other goods.

The household's choice is the optimum amount of housing to hold. If we insert the budget constraint into the utility function, we can write

$$U = \ln[y - (r + \delta) p^H H] + \eta \ln H$$

Taking the first-order condition for a maximum, we obtain

$$\frac{\partial U}{\partial H} = -\frac{(r+\delta)p^H}{Y-(r+\delta)p^H H} + \frac{\eta}{H} = 0$$

This condition can be rearranged to solve for the household's demand for housing:

$$H^D = \frac{\eta y}{p^H(r+\delta)(1+\eta)} \tag{9.18}$$

In the short run, the supply of housing is fixed at H^S. In equilibrium, demand will equal supply, so that $H^S = H^D$. This implies in turn that the equilibrium price of housing is

$$p^{H,*} = \frac{\eta y}{(r+\delta)(1+\eta)H^S}$$

Hardly surprisingly, the price will decrease with the short-run supply of houses H^S. Clearly, the greater the existing stock of houses, the lower the price. A more interesting implication of the result above, and one that is constantly relevant for millions of households, is the fact that the equilibrium price of houses decreases with the interest rate r. An unexpected lowering of the interest rate, perhaps due to a monetary policy intervention by the central bank, will lead to a shift in the demand curve outwards and a temporary excess demand for housing. This will eventually cause house prices to rise to a new and higher level ($p^{H,**}$), as illustrated in Figure 9.1.

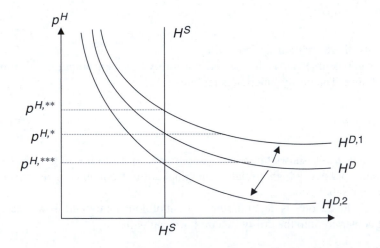

Figure 9.1 Equilibrium price of housing following falls in interest rates and in income.

Note also the impact of a fall in household income y, perhaps due to an economy-wide recession. In the short run, prices will typically be slow to adjust from the initial level $p^{H,*}$ and there will be an excess supply of houses that will be empty. Just like with wages, house prices tend to be sticky downwards. A price decrease means that household wealth for homeowners decreases and people will be reluctant to sell houses at a lower price than they paid for them (or for a lower amount than the household has used as collateral for loans for consumption, as in the United States). Hence, downward adjustment will be slow. The price should eventually settle at the new lower equilibrium level $p^{H,***}$.

10 Unemployment and the Labor Market

Having discussed capital accumulation, we now move on to discuss the other major physical factor of production: labor. The market for capital and the market for labor are remarkably different. Whereas capital markets are generally assumed to be working fairly efficiently in developed countries so that demand usually matches supply, this is not at all the case with labor markets. In fact, labor markets are rarely characterized by a situation where labor demand equals labor supply. Since Keynesian times, there has been a notion that different types of market failures typically affect the labor market, as will be discussed below.

The three main topics treated in this chapter are the theory of *efficiency wages*, associated with Shapiro and Stiglitz (1984), *insider–outsider* models of wage setting, and the *search and matching* framework developed by Peter Diamond, Dale Mortensen, and Christopher Pissarides.

10.1 Labor market disequilibrium

As shown in Chapter 6, both the demand and supply of labor will depend on the prevailing wage rate. Let $L^D(w)$ be firms' total demand for working hours (or workers), which is a function of the wage rate such that $\frac{\partial L^D(w)}{\partial w} < 0$.[1] Equivalently, let total labor supply be $L^S(w)$ such that $\frac{\partial L^S(w)}{\partial w} > 0$. If labor were a "normal" market, we would have a situation where $L^D(w^*) = L^S(w^*)$ at an equilibrium wage rate w^*. The standard situation in countries around the world is, however, that the prevailing wage rate is $\tilde{w} > w^*$, with the implication that $L^D(\tilde{w}) < L^S(\tilde{w})$, as shown in Figure 10.1. This excess supply, equal to $L^S(\tilde{w}) - L^D(\tilde{w}) = \mu$, is what we normally call *unemployment*.

Why is it that wage rates are set at levels too high for an equilibrium to occur? This is the issue that unemployment theory has been primarily concerned with. In the Keynesian paradigm, wages were modeled as being "sticky" in the downward direction but flexible upwards. Keynesian theorists tended to emphasize that the labor market was very special since it provided a livelihood for the vast majority of a country's population.

In the sections below, we will discuss three major explanations advanced in the literature: firms pay high wages in order to motivate workers and reduce shirking

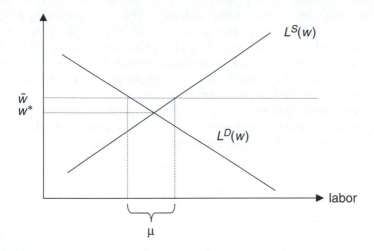

Figure 10.1 Unemployment.

(*efficiency wage theory*); firms want to cut wages but are prevented from doing so by contracts and labor unions (*insider–outsider theory*); and unemployment is largely due to worker heterogeneity and the substantial problem of allocating workers to suitable jobs (*search and matching models*).

10.2 Efficiency wages

The key assumption in efficiency wage theory is that the wage rate affects individual worker behavior. More specifically, it is assumed that a higher wage will induce workers to work harder, or to exert more effort. There may be several reasons why this is true. In developing countries, a higher wage means higher and more stable food consumption, which in turn has a direct effect on effort. In more advanced countries, a key link is that workers' true effort is hard for firms' managers to monitor. If workers could easily get a similar job elsewhere for the same wage, they would have an incentive to shirk on the job. A wage somewhat higher than necessary would thus make shirking – and the associated risk of getting fired – more costly for the individual worker. A third reason might be that higher wages improve the quality of job applicants. A higher wage might also build loyalty among workers and to the firm, whereas lower wages cause anger and shirking.

A very simple formulation of these ideas (which follows the exposition in Romer 2005) is to assume a firm with a profit function

$$\Pi = F(eL) - wL \tag{10.1}$$

where $F(eL)$ is the firm's production function, eL is "effective" labor, w is the wage rate, and L is the number of people employed. Labor is the only factor of production and the price of the goods produced is normalized to unity so that $F(eL)$ is the firm's total revenue. The production function has the standard features $F'(eL) > 0$ and $F''(eL) < 0$. The key assumption in the model, however, is that effort reacts to the wage level according to a function $e(w)$ where $e'(w) > 0$. Hence, the wage has both a negative and a positive impact on firm profits: on the one hand, it constitutes a direct cost in terms of wage payments; on the other hand, it increases net revenue due to a greater worker effort.

The firm's maximization problem is to choose the level of the wage w and the number of people employed L so as to maximize total profits $\Pi = F(e(w)L) - wL$. The first-order conditions for maximum are

$$\frac{\partial \Pi}{\partial w} = F'(e(w)L)Le'(w) - L = 0 \tag{10.2}$$

$$\frac{\partial \Pi}{\partial L} = F'(e(w)L)e(w) - w = 0 \tag{10.3}$$

From (10.3), we find that $F'(e(w)L) = \frac{w}{e(w)}$. This might be interpreted as a modified version of the standard optimization criterion: that the marginal product of labor $F'(e(w)L)$ should be equal to the (effort-adjusted) marginal cost $\frac{w}{e(w)}$.

Substituting this expression back into (10.2) and rearranging terms yields the optimality condition

$$\frac{\tilde{w}}{e(\tilde{w})}e'(\tilde{w}) = 1 \tag{10.4}$$

The term on the left-hand side is the elasticity of effort with respect to the wage. The wage at which this equality holds is $\tilde{w}$. Whether such a wage can be found depends to a large extent on the character of the $e(w)$ function. Figure 10.2 shows one example where the efficiency wage equilibrium is $\tilde{w} > 0$.

The firm's labor demand is in turn implicitly given by the expression in (10.3).

10.3   The Shapiro–Stiglitz model

The model above gave an intuition for why firms might want to set wages at higher levels than would ensure an equilibrium in total demand and supply. The richer efficiency wage model below from Shapiro and Stiglitz (1984) allows us to analyze the determinants of individual behavior in more detail. Let us imagine that workers have an instantaneous utility function

$$U(w, e) = w - e \tag{10.5}$$

where w is the wage received and e is the effort exerted. Utility is a negative function of effort and a positive function of the wage. We further assume that individuals can either exert $e = 0$ or some positive level $e = \bar{e} > 0$. Regardless of behavior, there is a probability b per unit of time that the worker loses his or her job. In the case

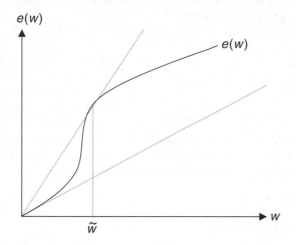

Figure 10.2 Example of an efficiency wage equilibrium.

of shirking, there is an additional probability $q > 0$ of being fired. Note that $q < 1$, which means that manager monitoring is imperfect; even in the case of shirking, there is a probability $1 - q$ that the worker will manage to keep his or her job. If the worker is unemployed, he or she will receive an unemployment benefit of $\bar{w}$. Workers are for simplicity assumed to maximize the expected present discounted value of utility over an infinite life. The interest rate is $r > 0$.

The key choice for the worker is whether to shirk or not. The lifetime utility from being an employed shirker is referred to as V_E^S, whereas the lifetime utility of an employed nonshirker is V_E^N. The so-called "fundamental asset equation" for shirkers shows that the interest rate times the "asset" V_E^S should be equal to the "flow benefit" at a point in time (equal to the wage w) minus the expected change in the value of the asset due to unemployment $(b + q)(V_E^S - V_U)$:

$$r V_E^S = w - (b + q)(V_E^S - V_U) \tag{10.6}$$

The interpretation of this condition is the following. V_E^S might be thought of as an asset that can be held by a worker. In order for it to be held by anyone, it should provide a rate of return during one unit of time equal to the market rate r. During that same unit of time, an individual is paid a wage w and faces a probability of $b + q$ of becoming unemployed. In the event of unemployment, the worker loses the difference between V_E^S and the lifetime utility of being unemployed, V_U. Since $V_E^S > V_U$, shirking might thus entail a "cost" $(b + q)(V_E^S - V_U)$. In equilibrium, (10.6) should be satisfied.

The lifetime utility of a nonshirking worker is V_E^N and the asset equation equivalent to the one above is

$$r V_E^N = w - \bar{e} - b(V_E^N - V_U) \tag{10.7}$$

In this case, the worker does not shirk and exerts an effort $\bar{e}$. Furthermore, the probability of being fired for shirking q is zero.

From these two equations, one can solve for the levels of V_E^S and V_E^N:

$$V_E^S = \frac{w + (b+q)V_U}{r+b+q} \tag{10.8}$$

$$V_E^N = \frac{w - \bar{e} + bV_U}{r+b}$$

A rational individual will not choose to shirk if $V_E^N \geq V_E^S$, a condition that we will refer to as the "no-shirking condition" (NSC). If we use the expressions in (10.8), a comparison between the two levels shows that

$$V_E^N \geq V_E^S \Longrightarrow$$

$$\frac{w + (b+q)\overline{V}}{r+b+q} \geq \frac{w - \bar{e} + bV_U}{r+b} \Longrightarrow$$

$$w + (b+q)V_U \geq (w - \bar{e} + bV_U)\left(1 + \frac{q}{r+b}\right) \Longrightarrow$$

$$\frac{-wq}{r+b} \geq (bV_U - \bar{e})\left(\frac{r+b+q}{r+b}\right) - (b+q)V_U$$

Multiplying both sides by $-(r+b)/q$ yields

$$w \geq (\bar{e} - bV_U)\left(\frac{r+b+q}{q}\right) + \frac{(b+q)(r+b)V_U}{q} \tag{10.9}$$

$$= \frac{(\bar{e} - bV_U)(r+b+q) + (b+q)(r+b)V_U}{q}$$

$$= \frac{\bar{e}(r+b+q)}{q} + rV_U$$

Expression (10.9) shows the wage that needs to be paid for workers not to shirk. All firms are aware of the NSC and hence set wages such that $V_E^N = V_E^S = V_E$ so that no shirking is carried out.

Given that $V_E^N = V_E^S = V_E$, we can equate the right-hand sides of (10.6) and (10.7) and insert V_E:

$$w - (b+q)(V_E - V_U) = w - \bar{e} - b(V_E - V_U) \Longrightarrow$$

$$V_E - V_U = \frac{\bar{e}}{q}$$

We can also rewrite the nonshirking asset equation (10.7) as

$$w = \bar{e} + rV_E + b(V_E - V_U) = \bar{e} + rV_U + (b+r)(V_E - V_U) \tag{10.10}$$

which will be useful later on.

What we still have not solved for is the lifetime utility of being unemployed, V_U. In an analogous manner as above, we can specify a fundamental asset equation for an unemployed individual as

$$r V_U = \bar{w} + a(V_E - V_U) \tag{10.11}$$

where $a > 0$ is the probability per unit of time that an unemployed worker finds a new job. As mentioned above, $\bar{w} > 0$ is the level of unemployment benefits.

Inserting (10.11) and the result that $V_E - V_U = \frac{\bar{e}}{q}$ into (10.10) gives us a closed-form solution to the wage rate that satisfies the NSC:

$$w = \bar{w} + \bar{e} + (a + b + r)\frac{\bar{e}}{q}$$

This critical wage increases with the required level of effort $\bar{e}$, with the interest rate r, with unemployment benefits $\bar{w}$, with the probability of finding a new job a, and with the probability of becoming unemployed b, and decreases with the probability that a worker who shirks is caught. The term $\bar{w}$ might be thought of as an indicator of the generosity of unemployment benefits. If unemployment benefits are high, workers have less to lose from being unemployed, and are therefore more prone to shirk. Hence, firms must pay higher wages. Likewise, if it is easy for an unemployed worker to find a new job, the expected cost of being unemployed is small, the worker is more willing to shirk, and a higher wage has to be paid.

What will the level of employment be? In a steady-state equilibrium, the number of people who become unemployed will be equal to the number of people who find new jobs. The number of workers who become unemployed at any given time is Lb, where L is the aggregate number of employed workers. The number of unemployed workers finding new jobs at any given time is $a(N - L)$. By setting these equal to one another and solving for a, we get $a = \frac{Lb}{N-L}$. This in turn implies that $a + b = \frac{Nb}{N-L}$. Further, $\frac{N-L}{N} = \mu$ is the unemployment rate in the economy, so the final NSC will be

$$w = \bar{w} + e + \left(\frac{b}{\mu} + r\right)\frac{\bar{e}}{q} \equiv \tilde{w}$$

All this is still on the supply side of labor. On the demand side, we will look at a representative individual firm, just as in the RBC model. Let us imagine that the firm has a production function $Q = F(L)$ so that the profit function is $\Pi = F(L) - wL$. Let us further assume that $F'(N) > \bar{e}$, i.e. if all potential workers were employed, they would still have a marginal product above the required effort level. Full employment would therefore be a good idea from the firm's point of view.

The usual profit maximization would give us the first-order condition $F'(L) = w$, as in the RBC model. In equilibrium the marginal product of labor must therefore be equal to the NSC, i.e. $F'(L) = e + (\frac{b}{\mu} + r)\frac{e}{q}$. This defines the equilibrium level of employment in the labor market. The higher the wage required to keep workers from shirking, the greater the level of unemployment. Workers who are unemployed would be willing to work for a wage below $\tilde{w}$, but cannot credibly commit to not shirking at that wage and hence are not employed.

10.4 Insider–outsider models

In Europe, it is commonly believed that union power could be an important reason for the higher levels of unemployment than in the United States. The intuition for understanding how unions affect unemployment is the assumption that unions care only about their own members, the *insiders*, who are already employed, and will aim for wage levels that are beyond a full employment equilibrium. The theory of insiders and outsiders in the labor market was pioneered by Lindbeck and Snower (1986).

To see this more formally, let us assume a representative firm with profits given by

$$\Pi = AF(L_I + L_O) - w_I L_I - w_O L_O$$

where A is some random productivity level to be defined below, L_I is employment of insiders, L_O is employment of outsiders, and w_I and w_O are their respective wage levels. The marginal products of insiders and outsiders are identical, $F_{L_I} = F_{L_O} > 0$, so that insider and outsider labor are perfect substitutes in production. We further assume that insider power manifests itself partly in the situation that $L_I = \bar{L}_I$, meaning that insiders are always employed for certain.

A is a random shift parameter, assuming value A_i with probability p_i. For simplicity, let us assume that $A_i = \{A_G, A_B\}$, where the good outcome is $A_G > A_B$, which happens with probability $p^G = p^B = 1/2$. Insiders only receive utility from their own wage level: $u_I = U(w_I)$, where $U'(w_I) > 0$.

Union bargaining power appears in two ways. Firstly, they are able to determine a linkage between their own wages and those that any outsider would get, $w_O = Rw_I$ where $R \in (0, 1)$. Unions are strong when R is high (or even equal to unity) since outsiders then cannot offer to work at a lower wage in order to enter the labor market. Secondly, insiders have a reservation utility u_0 below which they will go on strike. What is left for the firm to choose is therefore how many outsiders to employ, $L_{O,i}$, and the level of insider wages, $w_{I,i}$, at each state of the economy $i = G, B$.[2]

The maximization problem for the firm is

$$\max_{L_{O,i}, W_{I,i}} \sum_{i=G,B} p_i [A_i F(L_I + L_{O,i}) - w_{I,i} L_I - Rw_{I,i} L_{O,i}],$$

subject to $\quad \sum_{i=G,B} p_i U(w_{I,i}) \geq u_0$

The associated Lagrangian function is therefore

$$\Gamma = \sum_{i=G,B} p_i[A_i F(L_I + L_{O,i}) - w_{I,i}, L_I - Rw_{I,i}L_{O,i}]$$

$$+ \lambda \left(\sum_{i=G,B} p_i U(w_{I,i}) - u_0 \right)$$

By taking the first-order conditions with respect to $L_{O,i}$, $W_{I,i}$, we obtain

$$\frac{\partial \Gamma}{\partial L_{O,i}} = \frac{1}{2}[A_i F'(L_I + L_{O,i}) - Rw_{I,i}] = 0 \tag{10.12}$$

$$\frac{\partial \Gamma}{\partial w_{I,i}} = \frac{1}{2}[-(L_I + RL_{O,i}) + \lambda U'(w_{I,i})] = 0 \tag{10.13}$$

From (10.12), we find that the optimal level of outsider employment should satisfy $A_i F'(L_I + L_{O,i}^*) = Rw_{I,i}$, which is the standard result that marginal product should equal marginal cost. Comparing the good and the bad business cycle outcomes, we see that the left-hand side will be larger when $A_i = A_G$. Hence, in order to restore the first-order condition, $F'(L_I + L_{O,i}^*)$ must fall, which it can only do if $L_{O,G}^* > L_{O,B}^*$. Thus, firms will employ more outsiders in good times, which makes sense. Importantly, an increase in union power such that R increases must be balanced by an increase in $F'(L_I + L_{O,i}^*)$, which it can only do if $L_{O,i}^*$ falls. In this highly stylized sense, strong labor unions therefore increase unemployment.

From (10.13), we have another interesting implication. The first-order condition implies that $L_I + RL_{O,i} = \lambda U'(w_{I,i}^*)$ at the optimal insider wage rate $w_{I,i}^*$. Recall that if A_G prevails, then $L_{O,G}^*$ will be relatively high, which in turn means that $w_{I,G}^* < w_{I,B}^*$ (since marginal utility decreases with $w_{I,i}^*$). Thus, insider wages are countercyclical and will be higher in bad times. The intuition is that firms and insiders reach this decision jointly in order to keep outsiders from getting employed.

10.5 Search and matching models

Search and matching models, finally, focus on the fact that, unlike most other factors of production, workers are extremely heterogeneous. Matching the right person to the right job is indeed a complicated affair that frequently fails and could be a source of unemployment, according to theory.[3] Search and matching models were pioneered in works such as Diamond (1982) and Mortensen and Pissarides (1994). The account below relies on Acemoglu and Autor (2009).

Let us assume that new matches on the labor market M are created through a "matching function"

$$M(U, V) = \eta U^\beta V^{1-\beta}$$

where $\eta > 0$ is an efficiency parameter for new job creation, $U = \mu N > M$ is the number of unemployed people (the unemployment rate μ times the total size of the labor force L), and $V = vN$ is the number of vacancies in the economy (v is the vacancy rate). The number of employed people in the economy is $L = N - \mu N$. It is commonly assumed that the matching function displays constant returns to scale, i.e. it can be described as Cobb–Douglas. Note that a marginal increase in the number of unemployed will only increase the number of newly created jobs by $\beta M / U < 1$.

If we divide M through by the total labor force N, we can rewrite the expression as

$$m(\mu, v) = \frac{M(U, V)}{N} = \eta \mu^{\beta} v^{1-\beta}$$

The function $m(\mu, v) < 1$ should thus be thought of as the matching rate in the labor force as a whole, which is a function of the unemployment rate μ and the vacancy rate v.

Let us assume that we can describe the "tightness" of the labor market as $\theta = v / \mu$. θ relates the vacancy rate to the unemployment rate. If θ is low, this means that there are relatively few vacancies for every person unemployed. A low θ might thus be thought of as indicating a tight labor market where it is quite difficult to find a job.

Let us further define the (Poisson) arrival rate of a successful matching per vacancy as

$$q(\theta) = \frac{m(\mu, v)}{v} = \eta \left(\frac{\mu}{v} \right)^{\beta} = \eta \theta^{-\beta}$$

where $q'(\theta) = -\eta \beta \theta^{-\beta-1} < 0$. A Poisson process means that in some given short time interval Δt, the probability that one vacancy will be filled with one matched worker is $\Delta t \cdot q(\theta)$. This probability thus increases with the unemployment rate μ and with the length of the time interval Δt.

The Poisson arrival rate of a match for an unemployed worker is similarly

$$\frac{m(\mu, v)}{\mu} = \eta \theta^{1-\beta} = q(\theta)\theta \tag{10.14}$$

This function has some interesting properties. Let us assume that the time interval under consideration is $\Delta t = 1$. Then (10.14) shows the probability that an unemployed worker will find a job during one time unit. Consider now a small increase in the unemployment rate μ. In that case, the matching rate per vacancy $q(\theta)$ will increase. However, since there are also more unemployed people around to compete for the vacancies, the labor market has tightened and the net effect on the probability of finding a job is negative: $\partial(m(\mu, v)/\mu)\partial\mu = -\eta(1-\beta)\theta^{1-\beta}/\mu < 0$.

As in the Shapiro–Stiglitz model, the total number of jobs lost during a certain time interval is $bL = b(N - \mu N)$, where b shows the fraction of the employed who lose their jobs. *b* might be thought of as the probability that an individual worker succumbs to an exogenous shock during a short time interval Δt that makes her lose her job.

In equilibrium, it should be the case that the flow of people into employment is constant, $\dot{L} = \eta U^\beta V^{1-\beta} - bL = 0$. This also means that the number of jobs created through matching ($\eta U^\beta V^{1-\beta}$) should be equal to the number of jobs destroyed (bL). Dividing through by N, we obtain the equilibrium condition

$$\eta \mu^{*,\beta} v^{1-\beta} = q(\theta)\theta\mu^* = b(1 - \mu^*) \tag{10.15}$$

The endogenous variable in this equation is the unemployment rate μ^*. The unemployment rate that satisfies (10.15) is also a steady-state level. To see why, see Figure 10.3, which depicts job creation and job destruction as a function of μ. The $m(\mu, v)$ curve is positive and concave in μ whereas the job destruction curve is negative and linear.

If we start from a level $\mu > \mu^*$, then we see that more jobs are created through the matching process than are destroyed. This means that the unemployment rate μ should decrease. The situation is of course the reverse if $\mu < \mu^*$. Only at the steady-state level $\mu = \mu^*$ will the system be in equilibrium.

The schedule in Figure 10.3 can also be used for analyzing various comparative statics. Consider, for instance, an increase in the efficiency of matching η, perhaps as a result of a new government unemployment program. An increase in η will shift the $m(\mu, v)$ curve upwards at any given level of μ. The new steady-state level is now $\mu^{**} < \mu^*$. An increase in v would have a similar effect, whereas an increase in b would imply an increase in μ^*.

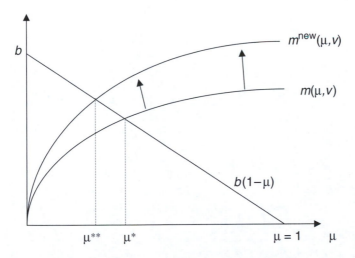

Figure 10.3 Equilibrium in the search and matching model.

The equilibrium condition in (10.15) can be used to draw the so-called *Beveridge curve*, showing the equilibrium relationship between the number of people unemployed U and the number of existing vacancies V (sometimes referred to as the *U–V curve*). Formally, the slope of the curve can be found by taking implicit derivatives of a function $B = \eta \mu^{*,\beta} v^{1-\beta} - b(1 - \mu^*) = 0$ created from the equilibrium condition in (10.15):

$$\frac{\partial \mu^*}{\partial v} = -\frac{\frac{\partial B}{\partial v}}{\frac{\partial B}{\partial \mu}} = \frac{-(1-\beta)\eta \mu^{*,\beta} v^{-\beta}}{\eta \beta \mu^{*,\beta-1} v^{1-\beta} + b} = \frac{-(1-\beta)\eta}{\theta(\eta \beta \theta^{1-\beta} + b)} < 0$$

A negative relationship is certainly well in line with intuition, since more vacancies should imply a lower rate of unemployment. This can also be deduced from Figure 10.3, where a higher level of vacancies implies a higher level of matching and a lower equilibrium unemployment rate. The negative association is well documented empirically for many countries in the world.

Part III
Macroeconomic Policy

11 IS–MP, Aggregate Demand, and Aggregate Supply

In this third part of the book, we will now shift our focus in order to analyze the effects of macroeconomic policy. Most of this chapter will be based on the IS–MP model of the goods and money markets. This model is not micro-founded since it is not based on optimizing household behavior. Instead, it follows in the Keynesian tradition of assuming certain behaviors of variables at the macro level. Only the specifications of aggregate supply will rely on micro foundations. The analysis in this chapter is therefore quite different from the analysis in most other chapters.

We start off with the traditional Keynesian framework where we discuss aggregate expenditure and multipliers. We then derive the aggregate demand function from equilibria in the goods and money markets. We also elaborate on the properties of the aggregate supply function under varying assumptions of price and wage stability and provide an overview of the *Lucas critique* of traditional Keynesian economic policy. After that, we present a new model that introduces financial intermediation into the standard IS–MP framework. Finally, we also present some of the main ideas in the so-called *new Keynesian* paradigm.

11.1 Aggregate expenditure and the multiplier

The traditional Keynesian model focuses to a great extent on *aggregate demand*. The typical starting point is an equation describing the user side of the economy. Let total output be Y, then total expenditure in a closed economy model (we assume away exports X and imports M) is $E_t = C_t + I_t + G_t$. In equilibrium, we should have that total expenditure equals total output so that $E_t = Y_t$. As noted in Chapter 8, the Keynesian consumption function is often described as $C_t = c_a + c_{\text{mpc}} Y_t^d = c_a + c_{\text{mpc}}(1 - \tau)Y_t$, where $c_a > 0$ is referred to as the *autonomous* part of consumption, which is independent of income, $c_{\text{mpc}} \in (0, 1)$ is the *marginal propensity to consume* (MPC), τ is the (percentage) income tax rate, and Y^d is disposable income, net of taxes.

The second component on the user side, gross investment I_t, is given by a function $I_t = i_0 - i_1 r$. i_0 is simply the intercept of this function when the real interest rate r is zero. The main idea is that investment decreases with the real interest rate.[1] Government expenditure G_t is assumed to be independent of income. Taken together, this means that we can write

$$Y_t = E_t = c_a + c_{\mathrm{mpc}}(1 - \tau)Y_t + I_t + G_t$$

If we isolate income on the left-hand side and rearrange, we end up with

$$Y_t = \frac{1}{1 - c_{\mathrm{mpc}}(1 - \tau)}(c_a + I_t + G_t)$$

This well-known expression has two parts; *autonomous spending* $(c_a + I_t + G_t)$ and the *multiplier* $1/[1 - c_{\mathrm{mpc}}(1 - \tau)] > 1$. It shows how the equilibrium level of income (and output) will change with a change in autonomous spending. Of particular interest are the effects of an increase in government spending G_t. A one-euro increase in G_t will according to this model increase output by $1/[1 - c_{\mathrm{mpc}}(1 - \tau)] > 1$ euro. If we assume some concrete numbers, for instance that $c_{\mathrm{mpc}} = 0.5$ and that $\tau = 0.2$, then the multiplier is $1/[1 - 0.5(1 - 0.2)] = 5/3$, i.e. an increase in G_t by 1000 euros would increase total output by 1667 euros. Clearly, the higher is c_{mpc} and the lower is τ, the greater is the multiplier.

This multiplier effect is illustrated in Figure 11.1. The figure shows the classical *Keynesian cross*, where an equilibrium initially exists at Y^*. At this level, total aggregate expenditure equals total output (given by the 45° line). An increase in autonomous government spending from G_t to G'_t shifts the intercept and the curve upwards, keeping the slope intact. Total expenditure increases, which implies that total output and incomes must increase in order to restore equilibrium. When income increases, consumption rises too via the MPC, which increases expenditure even further. A new equilibrium is eventually found at an

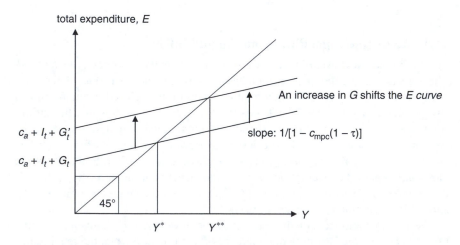

Figure 11.1 The Keynesian cross and the multiplier impact of an increase in government spending.

output level $Y^{**} > Y^*$. Note also that the multiplier effect implies that $G'_t - G_t < Y^{**} - Y^*$, i.e. equilibrium output will increase by a larger amount that the initial increase in G_t.

11.2   The IS–MP model

In this section, we will analyze short-run economic policy in the traditional Keynesian manner by assuming that prices are completely fixed. Rather than showing the more common IS-LM model, we make the modification here, as in Romer (2005), that we treat monetary policy as endogenous. Hence, "MP" replaces "LM" in the title, although most qualitative insights remain the same as in older models.

11.2.1   The goods market

The demand for goods is described by the well-known IS curve. It shows the combinations of output and the real interest rate where total output equals total expenditure, as discussed in the previous section. Real output is written as

$$Y = E(Y, r, G)$$

where we now use a general expenditure function $E(Y, r, G)$. E increases with output Y (through the consumption function) and with real government purchases G and decreases with the real interest rate r (for instance, since investments decrease with r). Should Y exceed total expenditures, actual production will be unused and inventories will accumulate.

We describe the partial derivatives with the following notation:

$$\frac{\partial E(\cdot)}{\partial Y} = E_Y > 0, \qquad \frac{\partial E(\cdot)}{\partial r} = E_r < 0, \qquad \frac{\partial E(\cdot)}{\partial G} = E_G > 0 \qquad (11.1)$$

We will assume that a one-dollar increase in disposable income increases planned expenditures by less than one dollar (as with the MPC) so that $E_Y < 1$.

As was mentioned above, the IS curve shows the combinations of Y and r where $Y = E(Y, r, G)$ applies. The slope of the curve can be found by differentiating with respect to r on both sides of the equality:

$$\left.\frac{dY}{dr}\right|_{IS} = E_Y \left.\frac{dY}{dr}\right|_{IS} + E_r$$

which after a bit of rearranging gives us

$$\left.\frac{dY}{dr}\right|_{IS} = \frac{E_r}{1 - E_Y}$$

Hence, the slope will be steeper the greater the sensitivities of planned expenditures to the real interest rate r and to changes in incomes Y are.

11.2.2 The money market

The money market means the market for the supply and demand of what is called "high-powered money", including currency (coins and notes) and reserves (on highly liquid bank accounts). The supply side of "real balances" is simply the total nominal stock of money, M, divided by the aggregate price level in society, P, measured for instance by a consumer price index.

The demand for real balances is determined by the nominal interest rate i, which we will here express as the real interest rate r plus expected inflation π^e so that $i = r + \pi^e$, and by the real level of income Y:

$$\frac{M}{P} = L(r + \pi^e, Y), \quad L_{r+\pi^e} < 0, \quad L_Y > 0 \tag{11.2}$$

The demand for money decreases with the nominal interest rate since the opportunity cost of holding money increases with the nominal interest rate that people would receive if they made more investments that are long-term.[2] In order to find the slope of the MP curve in (Y, r) space, consider an increase in r. If the equilibrium in (11.2) is to remain in place, the decrease in money demand must be balanced by an increase in Y. Hence, the MP curve will have a positive slope.

The key monetary policy variable is the real interest rate r, which is set by a central bank. This interest rate (often referred to as the "repo rate") is perfectly transmitted to the rest of the economy. In setting its interest rate, the central bank takes into consideration the output level Y as well as actual inflation π.[3] The behavioral rule is that central banks increase the real interest rate when output Y increases or when inflation rises. Hence, $r(Y, \pi)$ and the derivatives are $r_Y > 0$ and $r_\pi > 0$.

Reformulating (11.2) gives us an expression for the level of the nominal money supply, which will be endogenous to monetary policy:

$$M = PL(r(Y, \pi) + \pi^e, Y)$$

Note the distinction that monetary policy reacts to actual inflation levels π whereas the public, in this setting, adjusts its money demand through changes in expected inflation π^e.

11.2.3 Variations in IS–MP

The two curves can be drawn in the same diagram in (r, Y) space, as in Figure 11.2. As we have already derived, the IS curve is negatively sloped whereas the MP curve has a positive slope. Equilibrium in both markets occurs where the two curves cross. In standard Keynesian analysis, the effects of exogenous changes in policy variables are analyzed in this diagram.

As an example, we might consider an increase in government expenditure G. Such a change increases total expenditure, which means that the IS curve must shift outwards from the origin, as in Figure 11.2. For a given r, the level of output

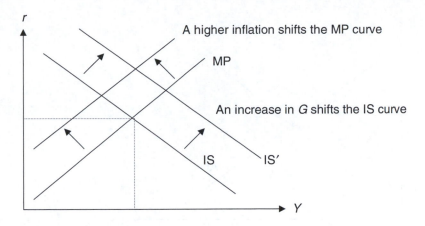

Figure 11.2 The IS–MP curves.

that satisfies an equilibrium in the goods market must be higher than before. The MP curve remains unaffected since government expenditures are assumed not to affect the aggregate price level in the short run. The outward shift in the IS curve implies a higher level of equilibrium output but also a higher interest rate, r.

11.3 Aggregate demand

The aggregate demand (AD) curve shows all the combinations of inflation levels and output where equilibria in the money and goods markets prevail simultaneously.[4] Since the AD curve is drawn with the level of inflation on the vertical axis and output on the horizontal axis, we now assume that prices are not completely fixed.

In order to see how the AD curve is derived from the IS–MP curves, consider an increase in the inflation rate, for instance due to a international oil shock. A rise in the inflation rate forces the central bank to increase the real interest rate. A higher r in turn increases the nominal interest rate, which reduces money demand. In the IS–MP diagram in Figure 11.2, a higher r at the same level of Y means that the MP curve shifts leftward and the two curves now cross again at a lower level of Y. The IS curve remains unaltered. Hence, a rise in π is associated with a fall in Y. This is the logic behind the negative slope of the AD curve in Figure 11.3.

To be able to say something more definite about the slope of the AD curve, we can start by differentiating the two equations behind the IS and MP curves with respect to inflation:

$$\left.\frac{dY}{d\pi}\right|_{AD} = E_Y \left.\frac{dY}{d\pi}\right|_{AD} + E_r \left.\frac{dr}{d\pi}\right|_{AD}$$

$$\left.\frac{dr}{d\pi}\right|_{AD} = r_\pi + r_Y \left.\frac{dY}{d\pi}\right|_{AD}$$

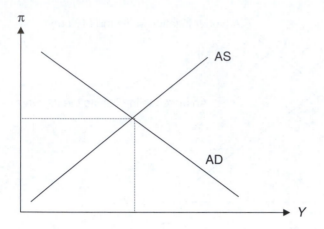

Figure 11.3 The AD–AS curves with sticky wages.

Inserting the second equation into the first gives us

$$\left.\frac{dY}{d\pi}\right|_{AD} = E_Y \left.\frac{dY}{d\pi}\right|_{AD} + E_r \left(r_\pi + r_Y \left.\frac{dY}{d\pi}\right|_{AD}\right)$$

$$\implies \left.\frac{dY}{d\pi}\right|_{AD} (1 - E_Y - E_r r_Y) = E_r r_\pi$$

$$\left.\frac{dY}{d\pi}\right|_{AD} = \frac{E_r r_\pi}{1 - E_Y - E_r r_Y} = \frac{r_\pi}{\left(\frac{1 - E_Y}{E_r} - r_Y\right)}$$

Since the numerator is positive while the denominator is negative, the expression as a whole will be negative, as shown in Figure 11.3.

Other changes in the components of the IS and MP curves will also have an impact on the AD curve. We discussed previously the effect of an increase in government expenditures G. The outward shift in the IS curve to a new equilibrium level of Y is associated with a simultaneous shift rightwards of the AD curve, since output increases at a given level of inflation.

11.4 Aggregate supply

11.4.1 Keynesian formulations with sticky wages

In the original Keynesian formulations, aggregate supply was primarily derived from the labor market. We saw in the RBC model how labor supply and demand determined the actual quantity of people employed in the economy as well as the output produced.

Let us imagine a representative firm whose only factor of production, for simplicity, is assumed to be labor. Its profit function is then

$$\Pi = PF(L) - wL$$

where P is the aggregate price level (equal to the firm's own price level), $F(L)$ is the production function with the usual properties $F'(L) > 0$ and $F''(L) < 0$, and w is the wage rate, which is fixed in the short run. The typical competitive firm will then hire up to the point when marginal revenue equals marginal cost: $PF'(L) = w$. Rewriting this equilibrium condition gives

$$F'(L) = \frac{w}{P}$$

To see the link to the aggregate supply (AS) curve, consider an increase in inflation π. Such an increase will involve a rise in P, which in turn means that the real wage falls (since the nominal wage w remains constant). In order to preserve equilibrium, the marginal product on the left-hand side must also fall, which it can do if L rises to some $L^1 > L$. If firms hire more labor, they can further produce more output so that $F(L^1) > F(L)$. Hence, there emerges a positive relationship between inflation and output. This is the reason for the positive slope of the AS curve in Figure 11.3.

11.4.2 The Phillips curve

Macroeconomic policy from the Second World War until the early 1970s was partly founded on the notion that there existed a permanent trade-off between unemployment and inflation for policy-makers to exploit. In order to derive such a relationship explicitly, let us use the same model as in the section above and make the additional assumption that the wage rate at time t is proportional to the price level from last year, P_{t-1}. More specifically, the relationship is

$$w_t = \gamma P_{t-1} \tag{11.3}$$

where $\gamma > 0$ is a constant describing the strength of the relationship. The equilibrium condition for labor demand is then

$$F'(L_t) = \frac{w_t}{P_t} = \frac{\gamma P_{t-1}}{P_t}$$

Since $\pi_{t-1} = \frac{P_t - P_{t-1}}{P_{t-1}} = \frac{P_t}{P_{t-1}} - 1$, we know that $\frac{P_{t-1}}{P_t} = \frac{1}{1+\pi_{t-1}}$. Thus, we can write

$$F'(\tilde{L}_t) = \frac{\gamma}{1 + \pi_{t-1}} \tag{11.4}$$

As mentioned above, an increase in inflation therefore increases the number of people employed in the next period. If the total labor force is N_t, then unemployment is $N_t - \tilde{L}_t = \mu N$. A rise in inflation in this way decreases the level of unemployment. This stable negative relationship between unemployment and inflation is famously referred to as the *Phillips curve* (Phillips 1958). The existence of exploitable Phillips curves has been a field of intense empirical research in recent decades.

11.4.3 The natural rate of unemployment

By the 1970s, it was fairly clear that a permanently exploitable Phillips curve did not appear to be in place. Friedman (1968) and Phelps (1968) argued, for instance, that a shift in policy towards a higher level of inflation with the aim of keeping unemployment low could not in the longer run keep wages from increasing. Rational workers would see through the Phillips curve reasoning and would not accept persistent decreases in their real wage. In terms of our model, this means that it is not likely that workers would accept a wage-setting rule according to (11.3).

The implication of this type of reasoning is that in the longer run, there should be a normal or *natural rate of unemployment* – sometimes referred to as the nonaccelerating inflation rate of unemployment (NAIRU) – from which monetary or fiscal policy could not diverge. Short-run deviations might be possible, as indicated by the short-run Phillips curve (SRPC) in Figure 11.4, but in the longer run there should not be an exploitable relationship between inflation and unemployment.

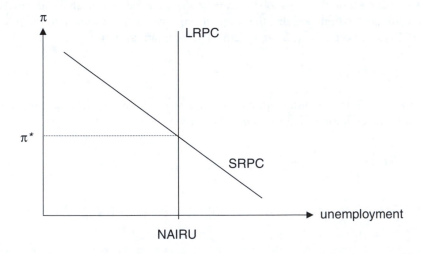

Figure 11.4 Short- and long-run Phillips curves.

The level of output associated with the natural rate of unemployment is $\bar{Y}$, often referred to as *long-run aggregate supply* or *the natural rate of output*. As with the LRPC, the long-run aggregate supply curve is vertical.

11.4.4 Expectations-augmented Phillips curves

In this section we discuss Keynesian reformulations of the Phillips curve based on later empirical evidence. It should be noted that the equations in this section are not micro-founded but should be seen as "reduced-form" equations that are primarily designed to be tested empirically.

If we incorporate the new assumptions about a natural rate of output, we might express an expectations-augmented Phillips curve (drawn in (π, Y) space this time) in the following manner:

$$\pi_t = \pi_t^* + \lambda(\ln Y_t - \ln \bar{Y}_t) + \epsilon_t \qquad (11.5)$$

Actual inflation π_t is thus a function of the "underlying" or "core" inflation π_t^* and of the log deviation between actual output Y_t and the natural rate of output $\bar{Y}_t$. There is also a random error term ϵ_t to incorporate the possibility of supply shocks. $\lambda > 0$ describes how strongly inflation reacts to output deviations from the long-run level. Note that if output is at its long-run level, the level of inflation will be π_t^* (in the absence of random shocks).

How is π_t^* determined according to this model? In the simplest case, it is just $\pi_t^* = \pi_{t-1}$. In this situation, it is implicitly assumed that individuals only react to changes in monetary policy with a time lag. The assumption also implies that there is a trade-off between *changes* in inflation rates and output (since we can write $\pi_t - \pi_t^* = \lambda(\ln Y_t - \ln \bar{Y}_t) + \epsilon_t$).

If individuals are fully rational and forward-looking, however, a more proper formulation would be $\pi_t^* = E_{t-1}(\pi_t)$, where $E_{t-1}(\pi_t)$ is the expected inflation one period back. In this setting, individuals would make their decision based on all available information about current and past policy choices when they make an expectation about inflation.

Sometimes the two differing views above are combined by assuming that $\pi_t^* = \phi E_{t-1}(\pi_t) + (1 - \phi)\pi_{t-1}$, where $\phi \in [0, 1]$ is a parameter. $\phi < 1$ implies that although people form rational expectations about the inflation rate, there is some degree of *inertia*, so that there is a connection between core inflation and past levels which goes beyond rational expectations. The source of such an inertia is often left unexplained.

11.4.5 Lucas supply curve

The models above simply assumed that there was some form of price or wage stickiness, in the literature often referred to as *nominal rigidities*. The exact source of such nominal rigidities is usually not discussed in the traditional macro literature.

Lucas (1972, 1973) developed a very influential model in which producers observe the price of their own good P_i but cannot observe the overall aggregate price level P. If the relative price P_i/P increases, for instance, the producer cannot therefore know if it is caused by a change in P_i, in which case a rational producer should increase production, or a fall in the aggregate price level, which should leave production unaffected. Due to this imperfect information scenario, the producer in Lucas's model will choose to increase output at least a little to stay on the safe side. Hence, there is also here a positive relationship between inflation and output.[5]

However, the key result from the model (which we do not derive here) is a micro-founded reformulation of the expectations-augmented Phillips curve:

$$\ln Y - \ln \bar{Y} = b[p - E(p)]$$

In this expression, $\ln Y$ is the log of actual output, $\ln \bar{Y}$ is the log of long-run aggregate supply, p reflects the (log of) the aggregate price level, $E(p)$ is the expectation of the aggregate price level, and $b > 0$ shows the sensitivity of output to deviations from the expected level of inflation. The key insight is once again that output will only deviate from the natural level if there is a surprise in the level of inflation. If, for instance, people expect monetary policy to be expansionary and their expectations are fulfilled, then $p - E(p) = 0$ and output remains at the natural rate.

This critique of the traditional Keynesian models has important implications for policy. In a very similar manner to the PIH model where individuals formed rational expectations about future incomes, the fact that people have rational expectations here will make economic policy based on output–inflation trade-offs very difficult. Nonsurprising monetary policy measures might even be harmful since they will increase inflation without affecting output or unemployment. In general, people will anticipate policy and adjust accordingly in advance. This general critique of how the lack of micro foundations in Keynesian analysis tends to make policy conclusions based on historical data problematic is often referred to as the *Lucas critique*.

11.5   Financial intermediation

In the IS–MP models discussed above, financial intermediaries such as banks do not play any role. Still, a lesson from the financial crisis of 2007–08 was that the functioning of the financial system might have important consequences for the real economy. In this section we present an extension of the IS–MP framework, proposed by Woodford (2010), that introduces financial intermediation into the standard model.

Let us assume that inflation expectations are now given throughout. For simplicity, we set $\pi^e = 0$ so that the nominal interest rate equals the real interest rate, $i = r$.

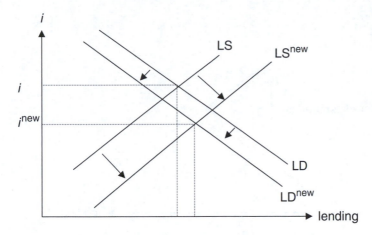

Figure 11.5 Impact of an increase in income on household demand and supply of lending.

As above, the IS curve is defined as the combination of the real interest rate r ($=i$) and total income Y, where total income equals total expenditure $E(Y, r)$, but let us now assume that we have no government. Total expenditure will thus be spent on consumption and investment, and savings should equal investment.

Unlike before, we derive the slope of the IS curve through the supply and demand of household lending. In Figure 11.5, we have drawn household demand for lending LD as a negative function of the nominal interest rate i. Similarly, households' supply of lending (i.e. savings) increases with the nominal interest rate. Without any credit market frictions, supply will equal demand at the rate i.[6]

If there is an exogenous increase in income Y, how will this affect the supply and demand for lending? Firstly, if all households have somewhat more income, they should be able to increase lending supply. The LS curve therefore shifts down to the right. The demand for loans should fall as incomes increase, but by a smaller amount. Hence, the LD curve shifts down to the left. The result is a lower equilibrium interest rate $i^{new} < i$ and a higher level of lending than before. We have thereby shown that there must be a negative relationship between Y and i for the goods market to be in equilibrium.

However, the analysis on the basis of Figure 11.5 assumes no credit market frictions, and there is no need for financial intermediaries since the supply of credit always meets demand. Let us now introduce a situation where financial intermediaries are necessary for effectively channeling credit (and perhaps for pooling risks, as shown in Chapter 7). In order to finance their activities, the financial intermediaries (we henceforth refer to them as banks) set a higher interest rate for borrowing i^b than for lending i^s, as in Figure 11.6a. The difference is referred to as the *credit spread* $\omega \geq 0$.

(a) *i*

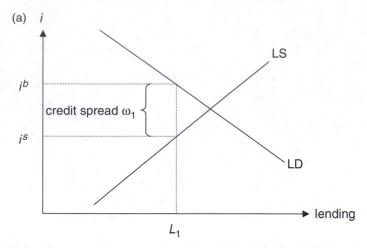

(b) ω

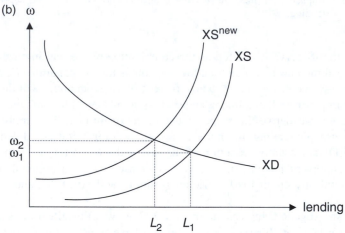

Figure 11.6 (a) Introducing financial intermediaries and credit supply frictions. (b) Supply and demand for financial intermediation as a function of the credit spread.

The supply and demand for financial intermediation is shown in Figure 11.6b and is a function of the credit spread ω. Clearly, if the credit spread is large, the interest rate on savings will be low and the demand for lending will also be relatively low. The reverse holds if the credit spread is low. On the other hand, a large credit spread should increase the number of firms willing to act as banks. The supply of financial intermediation is a positive function of ω since it is more profitable to be a bank when the difference between savers' and borrowers' interest rates are large. For a given level of ω, financial innovations or productivity increases would shift the XS schedule to the right whereas, for instance, tighter banking regulations such as a higher capital requirement (the bank's equity as a share of total assets including its lending) would shift the XS curve to the left. The equilibrium credit spread is initially given by ω_1 when the two curves intersect. The level of lending is then L_1.

Let us now consider the effects of a sudden reassessment of the total value of the banking system's assets, i.e. its lending to businesses and individuals.[7] A natural requirement for banks when risks increase would be to try increase the credit spread ω. For a given level of lending, this would be equivalent to shifting the XS curve to the left, as in Figure 11.6a to XS^{new}. The result is an increase in the equilibrium credit spread to ω_2 and a decrease in the amount of lending in the economy to L_2.

The increase to ω_2 implies that i^s must fall and that households' supply of lending to the banking system falls to L_2. In Figure 11.7, we draw the IS and MP curves in (i^s, Y) space instead of in (r, Y) space as above. The MP curve is given by $M/P = L(r(Y, \pi) + \pi^e, Y) = L(i^s(Y, \pi), Y)$ since we have assumed that $\pi^e = 0$. Furthermore, money demand $L(i^s(Y, \pi), Y)$ is a function of the interest rate on savings i^s rather than of i^b. People are more willing to convert their long-term assets into cash or cashable deposits if the interest rate on savings is low. The monetary policy rule by the central bank $i^s(Y, \pi)$ is targeted at i^s and stipulates that i^s increases with both Y and π as before. If this rule does not change, the MP curve will not shift as a result of the contraction of the XS curve.

The IS curve will, however, be affected by the change. For a given level of Y, i^s is now lower than before due to the increase in the required credit spread. The IS curve will therefore shift down, as in Figure 11.7. In equilibrium, there is a contraction of GDP. Hence, even without changes in monetary policy, a disturbance in the credit markets can have real effects via the IS curve.

In terms of the 2008 crisis, the model above seems to suggest that a downward spiral in credit supply and economic activity ensued after the initial shock. The

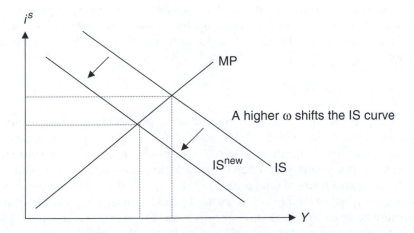

Figure 11.7 Impact of an increase in the credit spread.

contraction of GDP that was caused by the initial reassessment of banks' assets probably led to an even further shift of the XS curve to the left, which put pressure on i^s to fall even further. The IS curve thus also continued to fall to the left. As a response, the central banks kept lowering interest rates according to their policy rule, but eventually the level $i^s = 0$ formed a limit to effective monetary policy based on steering the real interest rate.

11.6 New Keynesian models

The Lucas critique and, even more so, the RBC paradigm both suggest that changes in nominal variables such as the money stock should not have real effects. According to the *new Keynesian* view, there might actually be good microeconomic reasons for nominal rigidities and such rigidities might matter for the real economy.

Consider, for instance, the assumption that there is a small cost associated with a change in prices. In line with Mankiw (1985), we might think of such a cost as arising from having to print new menus in the case of a restaurant. Let us assume a market structure with some degree of monopolistic competition so that there are many price-setting firms that find their optimal production level by setting marginal revenue equal to marginal cost. Actual demand is revealed after quantities have been set.[8] If, for instance, the demand for a product decreases, a profit-maximizing producer should decrease its price.

However, if there is a *menu cost* for changing prices, the producer must compare the loss in profit from keeping the price at the existing level, to the small cost of changing the price. If the loss is smaller than the menu cost, a rational producer should not change the price. Hence, in this case, there are good microeconomic reasons for price rigidity.[9]

In macro models of the aggregate price level, such price rigidity can be modeled by assuming that only a fraction of firms adjust their price to the profit-maximizing level. The remaining firms simply keep the price that they charged last period.

A particularly simple formulation used by, for instance, Gali and Gertler (2007) is that during some period t, the actual (log) price level p_t is determined by an equation

$$p_t = \theta p_{t-1} + (1 - \theta) p_t^*$$

The parameter θ should here be interpreted as the probability that firms *cannot* adjust their price during period t. With probability $1 - \theta$, firms are able to adjust their price to the profit-maximizing level. θ can thus be regarded as a measure of the degree of price rigidity. It follows that each firm is expected to maintain its price level for an amount of time equal to $1/(1 - \theta) > 0$. If $\theta = 2/3$, for instance, then firms only adjust their prices every third period. The adjusted price level p_t^* will in turn be given by a mark-up over current and future expected marginal cost since new Keynesian models typically assume that markets are characterized by imperfect competition.

12 Public Finance and Fiscal Policy

Fiscal policy concerns a government's handling of its revenues and expenditures. Typically, there is an imbalance between revenues and expenditures, which, in the case where expenditures exceed revenues, is referred to as a *budget deficit*. Budget deficits are measured on an annual basis and are usually described as a percentage of GDP. Accumulated budget deficits make up *government debt*, which is a stock variable that can be measured at any point in time and is also described as a percentage of GDP.

12.1 The government budget identity

The government budget identity at some point in time t shows the expenditures on the left-hand side and sources of finance on the right-hand side in the following manner:

$$G_t + r_t D_t \equiv T_t + \Delta D_t + \Delta M_t \tag{12.1}$$

In this expression, G_t is government expenditures in period t, $r_t D_t$ gives the real interest rate r_t times total accumulated government debt D_t, T_t is total tax revenue, $\Delta D_t = D_{t+1} - D_t$ is the change in the stock of government debt, and ΔM_t is the change in the money stock that is used for financing the government deficit.

Starting with the expenditure side, it simply consists of government outlays and interest payments. If the debt is high, interest payments will make up a large proportion of total expenditures. On the right-hand side, the main part of government spending should be financed by taxes T_t, but since these are not always sufficiently high to cover expenditures, governments often run budget deficits that increase its debt, $\Delta D_t > 0$. Irresponsible governments sometimes also try to cover deficits by "printing money", i.e. ordering the central bank to print new money that is then handed over to the government. In developed countries, this rarely happens and we will assume for now that $\Delta M_t = 0$.[1]

Rewriting (12.1) gives us an expression for the dynamics of the government budget deficit:

$$\Delta D_t \equiv (G_t - T_t) + r_t D_t$$

The term in parentheses is often referred to as the *primary deficit*. Budget deficits imply that $\Delta D_t > 0$, whereas budget surpluses imply a decreasing stock of debt $\Delta D_t < 0$. Note that in countries with very large debts (and hence large interest payments), even a moderate primary surplus $(G_t - T_t < 0)$ might not be enough for the debt to shrink.

Budget deficits are typically financed by governments' issuing of *bonds* that are sold to households and that give their holder an interest rate of r_t every year. If the total debt is bond-financed, D_t will be equivalent to the value of the stock of all outstanding bonds.

Over the long run, it is often assumed that government revenues and expenditures should add up. A "sustainable" long-term fiscal policy should thus satisfy:

$$\sum_{t=1}^{\infty} \frac{G_t}{(1+r_t)^t} + D_0 \leq \sum_{t=1}^{\infty} \frac{T_t}{(1+r_t)^t} \tag{12.2}$$

where r_t is the real interest rate as before. In other words, over an infinite time horizon, the present value of the flow of future government expenditures, plus some initial debt level D_0, should not exceed the present value of the flow of all future tax revenues. We will return to this intertemporal constraint below.

12.2 Ricardian equivalence

Should budget deficits be financed by higher taxes or by bonds? This is the central issue in the literature on *Ricardian equivalence*, pioneered by Barro (1974). As we shall see, the model is similar in spirit to the permanent income hypothesis of aggregate consumption.

The analysis of Ricardian equivalence starts off with an assumption about an infinitely lived representative household's intertemporal budget constraint:

$$\sum_{t=1}^{\infty} \frac{c_t}{(1+r_t)^t} \leq d_0 + \sum_{t=1}^{\infty} \frac{y_t - \tau_t}{(1+r_t)^t} \tag{12.3}$$

The present value of a lifetime of consumption expenditures should not exceed the present value of the infinite flow of disposable incomes (labor income y_t minus income taxes τ_t) plus the initial stock of bonds d_0. If the the economy is made up of L identical individuals, we can express the individual's constraint in (12.3) in terms of $C_t = c_t L$, $D_0 = d_0 L$, $Y_t = y_t L$, and $T_t = \tau_t L$.

When (12.2) holds with equality, we know that $\sum_{t=1}^{\infty} T_t/(1 + r_t)^t = \sum_{t=1}^{\infty} G_t/(1+r_t)^t + D_0$. Inserting this expression into (12.3) gives us

$$\sum_{t=1}^{\infty} \frac{C_t}{(1+r_t)^t} \leq \sum_{t=1}^{\infty} \frac{Y_t}{(1+r_t)^t} - \sum_{t=1}^{\infty} \frac{G_t}{(1+r_t)^t}$$

In this way, we can express the households' budget constraint as a function of the present value of government expenditures. The key thing to notice is that the time path of taxation does not enter the equation above. The financing of deficits with bonds or taxes should therefore not matter to households. This is indeed the Ricardian equivalence result. Only the quantity of government expenditures should matter for consumption over the long run.

The intuition behind this result is that households do not value bonds as net wealth. Consider the following example: From having a balanced budget with no debt at some time t, the government chooses to lower taxes T_t. G_t remains the same as before, but now $G_t > T_t$, so that debt accumulates. The government finances the deficit by selling bonds to the households. Will this increase in disposable income increase consumption? According to the Ricardian equivalence result, it will not because households realize that the long-term budget constraint is given by (12.2). At some point in time, governments will need to restore the satisfaction of the constraint by increasing taxes again. Hence, the increase in disposable incomes from the temporary tax decrease is saved in order to pay for the higher taxes in the future.

In this sense, the implications of Ricardian equivalence are very similar to those of the PIH model. The traditional Keynesian view would, however, hold that an increase in bond financing should increase consumption since it leaves households with a temporarily higher disposable income. Once again, there is thus a substantial difference in the predicted effects of government policy between the traditional Keynesian view and the view of rational, forward-looking households.

Ricardian equivalence is one of the most often discussed results in macroeconomics. A number of objections have been raised against Barro's hypothesis. For instance, it assumes (like the PIH model) that individuals have no liquidity constraints and can always save and borrow without difficulty. A second objection is that it is not likely that individual households will act in accordance to the infinite horizon budget constraint in (12.3). Rather, it is more likely that one generation (with a finite lifetime) will indeed react to medium-term expansionary fiscal policies since it is unrealistic to believe that they are perfectly altruistic towards future generations. Empirical evidence also seems to suggest significant departures from Ricardian equivalence.[2]

12.3 Tax smoothing

The Ricardian equivalence analysis above focused on households that reacted to exogenously set levels of taxes and government expenditures. But what determines the decisions of governments regarding budget deficits or surpluses? In standard microeconomic theory, it is shown that taxes are often associated with deadweight losses that reduce welfare. In this section, we assume in line with Barro (1979) a benevolent social planner who wishes to minimize the distortions caused by taxation, while still honoring the intertemporal budget constraint.

Let us assume, as before, that government expenditures G_t are exogenous to the model. Taxes give rise to distortionary costs for the economy equal to

$$Z_t = Y_t z\left(\frac{T_t}{Y_t}\right), \quad z'\left(\frac{T_t}{Y_t}\right) > 0, \quad z''\left(\frac{T_t}{Y_t}\right) > 0 \tag{12.4}$$

The expressions in (12.4) assume that the distortionary costs of taxation are an increasing and convex function of taxes as a share of GDP, T_t/Y_t (the tax quotient), scaled by the general size of the economy Y_t. The z-function provides a shortcut for the many different distortions that taxes give rise to but provides no information about their exact sources. No taxes implies zero distortions in this setting: $z(0) = 0$.

The intertemporal budget constraint that governments face is still given by (12.2). Hence, the optimization problem becomes

$$\min_{T_0, T_1 \dots} \sum_{t=1}^{\infty} \frac{Y_t}{(1+r_t)^t} z\left(\frac{T_t}{Y_t}\right) \quad \text{subject to} \quad \sum_{t=1}^{\infty} \frac{T_t}{(1+r_t)^t} = \sum_{t=1}^{\infty} \frac{G_t}{(1+r_t)^t} + D_0$$

As was the case in the PIH, the first-order condition for this problem gives us an Euler equation of the type $z'(\frac{T_t^*}{Y_t}) = z'(\frac{T_{t+1}^*}{Y_{t+1}})$, which in turn implies that optimally

$$\frac{T_t^*}{Y_t} = \frac{T_{t+1}^*}{Y_{t+1}}$$

In other words, distortionary costs are minimized when taxes as a share of GDP are smoothed over time. This is the *tax smoothing* result, with the same basic intuition as consumption smoothing.

Extending this model to include uncertainty is straightforward. In the case of a quadratic z-function (as in Hall's random-walk model), we will have

$$\frac{T_t^*}{Y_t} = E_t\left(\frac{T_{t+1}^*}{Y_{t+1}}\right)$$

Taxes as a share of GDP thus follow a random walk. The result suggests that at all points in time, the government includes all available information about expected future incomes and sets the current level of T_t/Y_t so that it is expected to be equal to all future levels of tax quotients. Any change from this pattern must be due to random new information.

12.4 Political economy of government debt

In the tax smoothing model above, tax policy is determined by a benevolent government that aims to minimize the distortionary effects of taxes. It does not have much to say about the dynamics of budget deficits. Over the infinite time horizon, the current value of total taxes will be equal to the current value of government spending, but in individual time periods there might be an imbalance. The benevolent government will, however, correct those imbalances sooner or later.

A less optimistic observer of fiscal policy around the world would probably argue that many governments' levels of deficits and debts cannot possibly be sustainable in the long run and cannot reasonably reflect expectations about potential future incomes. For instance, several countries around the world have levels of accumulated government debt above 100 percent of GDP at the same time as the future prospects for their economies appear bleak. Historically, it is well known that some countries have even gone "bankrupt" and have had to cancel or extensively reschedule their debt repayments.[3] Hence, it has been argued that long-term fiscal policy frequently is characterized by government failure.

A potential source of such failures is the political system itself. In a famous model, Alesina and Tabellini (1990) argue that in a democracy where two parties with different preferences over public goods compete for office, an incumbent party might strategically "overspend" while in office in order to constrain the fiscal choices for an opposing party should that party win office in the next period. The result of such a strategic use of government debt is a *deficit bias* in fiscal policy that is inefficient from a social point of view.

Consider a country with two political parties that we might refer to as left (L) and right (R). The parties do not disagree on the level of taxes but only on how to spend the taxes raised. The left-wing party wants to spend raised taxes only on public good $g_t^L \geq 0$, where t indicates the period in question, whereas the right-wing party prefers to spend on a different public good g_t^R. One might, for instance, think of g_t^L as general health care and g_t^R as military defense. In this simplified setting, there are only two time periods: period 1 and period 2. The identity of the incumbent party in period 1 is given and there is then an election at the beginning of period 2. The right-wing party is expected to win this election and rule in period 2 with an exogenously given probability of $\rho \in [0, 1]$. The probability of a left-wing victory in the election is thus $1 - \rho$.

The utility functions of the right- and left-wing parties, given that they are in power during the first period, are

$$V^R = u(g_1^R) + \beta[\rho u(g_2^R) + (1 - \rho)u(g_2^L)] \tag{12.5}$$

$$V^L = v(g_1^L) + \beta[(1 - \rho)v(g_2^L) + \rho v(g_2^R)]$$

respectively. The instantaneous utility functions $u(g_t^R)$ and $v(g_t^L)$ have the usual properties $u'(g_t^R), v'(g_t^L) > 0$ and $u''(g_t^R), v''(g_t^L) < 0$. Note also that $u(g_t^L) = v(g_t^R) = 0$, i.e. if the other party wins the election and provides its preferred public good, the losing party is assumed to yield no utility. $\beta \leq 1$ is the usual time discount factor.

The country earns an exogenous flow of per capita incomes during the two periods equal to $y_1, y_2 > 0$, where we assume $y_2 \geq y_1$. The income tax rate is $\tau < 1$, so that the intertemporal flow of government revenue is τy_1 and τy_2. The government starts off without any government debt. In the first period, the government in power might, however, incur a debt equal to d that must be repaid in full in period 2. These conditions imply that the budget constraints for party $j = R, L$ in power are

$$g_1^j = \tau y_1 + d$$

$$g_2^j = \tau y_2 - d$$

(12.6)

The party in power during period 1 thus maximizes (12.5) subject to (12.6). The choice variable that we are interested in is the level of debt chosen in the first period, d. The optimal level of debt can be found if we insert the expressions for (12.6) into the utility functions and then maximize with respect to d.

Let us, for instance, assume that the right-wing party is in power in period 1. The optimization problem for the government is thus

$$\max_d u(\tau y_1 + d) + \beta \rho u(\tau y_2 - d)$$

The first-order condition for this problem is

$$\frac{\partial V^R}{\partial d} = u'(\tau y_1 + d) - \beta \rho u'(\tau y_2 - d) = 0$$

With this general utility function, we are as always unable to calculate any explicit solutions, although it is certainly possible to carry out comparative statics with the help of implicit differentiation.

In order to derive an explicit solution, let us assume logarithmic utilities so that $u(g_t^R) = \ln g_t^R$ and $u(g_t^L) = \ln g_t^L$. In that case, the first-order condition tells us that

$$\frac{1}{\tau y_1 + d} = \frac{\beta \rho}{\tau y_2 - d}$$

By manipulating this expression, we can solve for the optimal level of government debt:

$$d^* = \frac{\tau(y_2 - \beta \rho y_1)}{1 + \beta \rho}$$

(12.7)

The key insight from this expression is that the optimal level of debt incurred by an incumbent party in the first period is negatively associated with the party's probability of winning the election in period 2. More formally, the derivative is

$$\frac{\partial d^*}{\partial \rho} = -\frac{(y_1 + y_2)\beta \tau}{(1 + \beta \rho)^2} < 0$$

Hence, if the right-wing party is the incumbent in period 1, the optimal debt will be smallest if $\rho = 1$, i.e. if the incumbent party is 100 percent sure of winning the next election. From (12.7), we can deduce that the debt will then be $d^* = \tau(y_2 - \beta y_1)/(1 + \beta) \geq 0$. Note that as long as $y_2 - \beta y_1 > 0$, the party in government will always opt for a positive amount of debt. The size of the debt increases with the growth in income, $y_2 - y_1$. Hence, it is more rational for fast-growing economies to have government debt than for slow-growing countries.

A straightforward corollary of the result above is that debt will be highest when the probability of re-election ρ approaches zero. If that is the case, we can see from the utility function that the party in power will discount the future by a factor $\beta\rho$ that will be close to zero. Since the party can only spend on the public goods that it likes in the first period, it will take on as much debt as possible in the first period. In the limiting case of $\rho = 0$, we can deduce from (12.7) that the optimal first-period debt will be τy_2, i.e. the debt will be so high that the opposing party that takes over has to spend all its government revenue on paying back the debt. If, for example, the right-wing party only cared for military spending, it would spend $\tau(y_1 + y_2)$ on the military in period 1 so that the left-wing party would not be able to spend anything on health care while in power in period 2.

Usually, the level of government debt is discussed in terms of shares of total GDP. If $y_1 = y_2 = y$, then optimal debt as a share of GDP is simply

$$\frac{d^*}{y} = \frac{\tau(1 - \beta\rho)}{1 + \beta\rho}$$

This expression highlights two other important factors for countries' willingness to accept government debt: the time discount rate β and the tax rate τ. Societies with more impatient individuals (a low β) are more likely to have high debt than societies with patient individuals. Similarly, it is only intuitive that high-tax countries (a high τ) with a large public sector will have higher debt as a share of GDP than low-tax countries.

12.5 Debt financing versus debt forgiveness

As indicated above, many countries in the world have levels of government debt that are not sustainable. In fact, there are several historical examples of situations where a government's international lenders have realized that the country's level of debt far exceeds the expected debt repayments in the future. What should lenders then do, in their own interest as well as in the interest of the indebted country? Should they continue to finance the debt with new loans, hoping that the country will be able to pay after all, or should they forgive some of their claims so that the level of debt stabilizes at a sustainable level?

The debt crisis among developing countries during the era of structural adjustment programs led to debt rescheduling and even debt forgiveness for some highly indebted countries. Since the financial crisis of 2007–08, the issue has become a particularly hot topic within the European Union, with countries like Greece and Portugal having difficulties in servicing their debts.

12.5.1 Debt overhang

In this section we briefly outline the influential analysis of the problem by Krugman (1988). The model assumes a two-period framework as above and that the country in question has inherited a level of debt equal to $d > 0$. The flows of government revenue during periods 1 and 2 are given by τy_1 and τy_2 where τ is an exogenously given tax rate and $y_1, y_2 > 0$ are levels of income. The debt can be paid back during both periods. The country can at most reduce its debt in the first period by τy_1, so that debt in period 2 is $d - \tau y_1 = b \geq 0$. If $b > 0$, international lenders might choose to refinance this amount at the prevailing international interest rate $r > 0$. The debt payment in the second period will then be $(d - \tau y_1)(1 + r)$.

Assume now that whereas first-period revenues are known with certainty, second-period revenues are uncertain and might take on either a high value y_2^H or a low value y_2^L, where $y_2^H > y_2^L$. The differences in income could, for instance, be due to high or low world market prices for the goods that the country is selling. Suppose that the probability of the good outcome is ρ and the probability of the bad outcome is $1 - \rho$. On top of this, actual revenue in period 2 might depend on government adjustment effort e. Adjustment efforts could, for instance, be an exchange rate realignment or the abolition of harmful tariffs that serve to improve the functioning of the economy and increase income. For simplicity, we assume that every unit of adjustment effort results in one additional unit of output. Taken together, the expected level of second-period government revenue in period 1 is therefore $E_1(y_2) = \rho y_2^H + (1 - \rho)y_2^L + e$ whereas the actual levels are

$$y_2 = y_2^i + e$$

where $y^i \in \{y^H, y^L\}$. We will return later to what determines the government level of effort e.

The country's expected maximum ability to pay in the second period is thus $\tau E_1(y_2) = \tau[\rho y_2^H + (1 - \rho)y_2^L + e]$. The country has an unsustainable level of debt in the second period if $b(1 + r) > \tau E_1(y_2)$. Equivalently, a country with an unsustainable level of debt (in Krugman's words a *debt overhang*) is characterized by a situation where

$$d > \tau y_1 + \frac{\tau E_1(y_2)}{1+r} = \tau y_1 + \frac{\tau[\rho y_2^H + (1 - \rho)y_2^L + e]}{1+r} \tag{12.8}$$

i.e. where the level of debt exceeds the expected present value of total future government revenue. A typical risk-neutral or risk-averse international lender would in general be reluctant to lend to such a country in the initial period. A result of a refusal to lend could be that the country has to default on its debt and cancel all repayments.

An obvious general solution to the debt overhang problem above would be to raise the proportional tax rate to a new level $\tau^{\text{new}} > \tau$ such that $\tau^{\text{new}} \geq d / \left(y_1 + \frac{E_1(y_2)}{1+r} \right)$. In developed economies in the Western world, this is certainly a feasible strategy that might at least partly overcome the overhang problem. However, as emphasized by Besley and Persson (2010), for instance, a country's *fiscal capacity* to tax its citizens is closely linked to its *legal capacity*, or more generally, to its *state capacity*. Some countries, for instance in Europe, developed such capacities over several hundreds of years, and states that were not able to tax their citizens effectively were often simply wiped off the map through military competition. Similar processes have not been in place in other parts of the world, particularly not in Africa where statehood is generally quite recent. Hence, the capacity to raise the level of τ might just not be in place in many parts of the world.

Even if this is the case, both the indebted country and the world community usually want to avoid episodes of *sovereign default*, although there are many instances of such events in history. Since it was founded in 1945, the *International Monetary Fund* (IMF) has acted as a lender of last resort to heavily indebted countries. By 2011, Greece was one of the countries that had to turn to the IMF for help to finance its government debt.

How should an optimal debt contract be designed? Clearly, a profit-maximizing financial institution would only care about its own expected profit and would not lend to a country with a debt overhang. Given that the IMF presumably gives some weight to the indebted country in its utility function, its optimal strategy will be different.

Let us consider the situation in period 1 and imagine that a liquidity crisis has emerged so that remaining debt payments exceed expected future government revenue, $b(1+r) > \tau E_1(y_2)$. What are the options for a lender like the IMF? To begin with, note that even if the debt is unsustainable according to the definition above, it might still be the case that $\tau(y_2^H + e) > b(1+r)$, i.e. the country might be able to pay back its debt if the good outcome y_2^H materializes. One strategy might therefore be to lend the full amount and hope for the good outcome to happen (or for government effort e to be sufficiently high) so that the IMF recovers all of its credit. The actual repayment q would then be:

$$q = \begin{cases} \tau y_2 & \text{if } \tau y_2 < b(1+r) \\ b(1+r) & \text{if } \tau y_2 > b(1+r) \end{cases} \tag{12.9}$$

If $q = \tau y_2$, the government must default on debt payments of the size $b(1+r) - \tau y_2 > 0$. The amount of tax revenue left for the government to spend on public goods other than debt repayments will in that case be $g_2 = \tau y_2 - q = \tau y_2 - \tau y_2 = 0$. If, however, $\tau y_2 > b(1+r)$, then $g_2 = \tau y_2 - b(1+r) > 0$.

A second strategy for the IMF might be to provide the loans but at an interest rate set lower than the international interest rate, $r^{\text{low}} < r$. One possible choice is simply to set the interest rate at a level such that the country just can pay back in the bad outcome:

$$q = (1+r^{\text{low}})b = \tau y^L \implies r^{\text{low}} = \frac{\tau y^L}{b} - 1$$

in which case the country's debt would in fact be sustainable. Actual payment, regardless of outcome, is then $q = \tau y^L$. However, this lower interest could be seen as a reward for irresponsible behavior and since the IMF would have to make up for the interest differential to the international interest rate $(r - r^{low})$, it would still be close to a government default.

A third and closely related strategy might be to reschedule or "forgive" some of the debt already in period 1 to a new level $b^{low} < b$ such that

$$q = (1+r)b^{low} = \tau y^L \implies b^{low} = \frac{\tau y^L}{(1+r)}$$

This is equivalent to a partial default by the government by an amount $(b - b^{low})(1+r)$ and is likely to make it hard for the country to borrow money on the international capital market in the future.

Why would the IMF ever choose the latter two alternatives when they clearly yield repayments that are smaller than or equal to the contingent payment in (12.9)? Note that in the two latter cases, government spending is either $g_2 = \tau y_2 - \tau y^L = \tau(y^H + e) > 0$ or $g_2 = \tau(y^L + e) \geq 0$. By setting a low level of repayment, the IMF gives governments stronger incentives for making necessary adjustment efforts e. In the subsection below, we formalize this idea further.

12.5.2   *Endogenous adjustment efforts*

What determines a country's adjustment efforts when it has been hit by a debt crisis? In line with the model in Krugman (1988), let us assume that the government has a very simple utility function such that it only has preferences over second-period government spending g_2 and its adjustment effort e (for instance, because the indebted country must always pay back τy_1 in the first period so that $g_1 = 0$ anyway). Government spending is given by $g_2 = \tau y_2 - q$, where q is the actual repayment that the government makes according to its contract with the IMF, as specified above.

The expected utility of second-period government consumption is given by a function $E_1(u(g_2))$ such that $u'(g_2) > 0$ and $u''(g_2) < 0$. The government gets disutility from making adjustment efforts e. Such necessary reforms typically imply that some groups in society lose as compared with before, perhaps due to labor market or pension reforms. This disutility is described by a function $v(e)$ with the properties $v'(e) > 0$ and $v''(e) > 0$ so that marginal disutility is increasing in e. Taken together, the expected utility of the government is given by

$$E_1(U) = E_1(u(g_2)) - v(e) \tag{12.10}$$
$$= [u(\tau[\rho y_2^H + (1-\rho)y_2^L + e] - q)] - v(e)$$

where we have substituted in $E_1(y_2) = \rho y_2^H + (1-\rho)y_2^L + e$ in the second line.

The government's control variable in this utility function is its level of adjustment effort e. It is easy to see that adjustment effort entails a trade-off. On the one hand, a higher e increases $E_1(y_2)$, which usually increases potential government spending g_2. On the other hand, the "marginal cost" of effort is $v'(e) > 0$. Note also that for all levels such that $\tau y_2 < b(1+r)$, the government has no incentive to increase its efforts since all extra government revenue will disappear in repayments to lenders.

To see this more formally, we can derive the first-order condition for an interior maximum on the basis of (12.10) to be

$$\frac{\partial E_1(U)}{\partial e} = u'(g_2)\frac{\partial E_1(g_2)}{\partial e} - v'(e) = 0$$

Since we know that $u'(g_2) > 0$ and $v'(e) > 0$ for all $e > 0$, the existence of a positive equilibrium level $e^* > 0$ will depend on the term $\partial E_1(g_2)/\partial e$. If the IMF does not forgive any debt, if it lends at the international interest rate r, and hopes for a positive outcome so that a full repayment can be made, then for all levels such that $\tau E_1(y_2) < b(1+r)$, the government is expected to earn $\tau E_1(y_2)$ and has to repay the same amount. A rise in e increases expected revenue and expected repayments one for one and hence $\partial E_1(g_2)/\partial e = 0$. Governments therefore have no incentive to make adjustment efforts and the optimal level is $e^* = 0$.

If the debt contract is set at the more generous level $q = \tau y^L$, then $\tau E_1(y_2) > q$ and extra efforts will increase $E_1(g_2)$ at all $e > 0$. This implies that $\partial E_1(g_2)/\partial e = 1$ and that the optimal level of effort is given by $u'(g_2) = v'(e^*)$. In this section, we have not explicitly modeled the utility function of the IMF, but is seems quite intuitive that an outcome where $e^* > 0$ might be part of its preference structure.

13 Inflation and Monetary Policy

Inflation is the percentage increase in the aggregate price level (usually measured by a consumer price index) from one year to the next. Inflation has been observed throughout history for as long as money has existed. The chapter will focus on the causes of inflation and analyze how monetary policy affects inflation and the economy as a whole.

At a general level, we saw in Chapter 11 that inflation will be heavily influenced in the short run by aggregate supply and aggregate demand. An expansion in demand, for example, always leads to an increase in inflation (unless the AS curve is horizontal). Negative supply shocks – for instance, due to a rise in the price of a key production factor like oil – will lead to a supply contraction and an increase in inflation.

In this chapter we will delve further into mainly the political economy of inflation and the perceived trade-off between inflation and output growth. We will start off with the classical *quantity theory of money* and then proceed with the *time-inconsistency model* of monetary policy and its potential solutions, originally associated with Kydland and Prescott (1977). After that, we move on to an extensive discussion of *political business cycles* and analyze how inflation is affected by the presence of political parties with different preferences for price stability. These sections will rely to a great extent on Alesina and Stella (2010). Finally, we include a treatment on *seigniorage*.

13.1 The quantity theory of money

In the long run, it is widely recognized that inflation has a very close association with money supply. The most general formulation of the *quantity theory of money* proposes the following basic relationship:[1]

$$MV = PY$$

In this equation, M is the nominal stock of money as before, V is the *velocity of money*, or the average frequency at which a unit of money is spent in an economy, P is the aggregate price level, and Y is real GDP. V is a parameter that does not change much over time and that depends among other things on a country's financial sector development. Y is usually also taken as given in this setting. Thus, the aggregate price level can be formulated as $P = M\frac{V}{Y}$. An increase in M will have a positive effect on P, i.e. there will be inflation. Especially over the long run, it has been well documented empirically that large increases in money supply tend to be followed by inflation.

13.2 Inflation and the money market

From Chapter 11, we know that equilibrium in the money market will prevail if real money supply equals real money demand such that

$$\frac{M}{P} = L(r + \pi^e, Y)$$

Rewriting this expression, and assuming for now that $\bar{Y}$ and $\bar{r}$ are constants and that the monetary policy rule does not apply, we get $P = M/L(\bar{r} + \pi^e, \bar{Y})$, i.e. just like in the quantity theory, there is a close association between the aggregate price level and the nominal money stock. Indeed, we will have that actual inflation and expected inflation are

$$\frac{\dot{P}}{P} = \pi = \pi^e = \frac{\dot{M}}{M}$$

where $\dot{P}/P$ and $\dot{M}/M$ are the growth rates (the time derivative divided by the current level) of the aggregate price index and the nominal money stock, respectively. Prices are thus completely flexible.

Let us consider the case when a monetary authority announces that it will increase the growth rate of money $\dot{M}/M$. This increase in turn increases actual as well as expected inflation $\pi = \pi^e$. Through its positive impact on the nominal interest rate $i = r + \pi^e$, the demand for money therefore shrinks immediately.[2] In order to balance the fall in money demand, real money supply must also fall, i.e. P must increase. Hence, the rise in the money growth rates both increases the inflation rate in the longer run and leads to a one-time discontinuous jump in the aggregate price level.

Analogously, if monetary authorities reduced money growth, there would be a decrease in long-run inflation but also an immediate discontinuous fall in the price level. In order to avoid such a dramatic scenario, central banks should combine the lowering of long-run money growth rates with a temporary increase in the level of money supply (Romer 2005).

13.3 Time inconsistency in monetary policy

Although the quantity theory and money market analysis above highlights the close association between money supply and inflation, it does not answer the question of why central banks or governments choose to maintain too high a level of money growth. The remaining sections deal primarily with this issue.

From the analysis of Phillips curves in Chapter 10, we know that a plausible explanation for persistently high levels of inflation is the perceived trade-off between inflation and unemployment. In a famous article, Kydland and Prescott (1977) argued that even without a long-run output–inflation trade-off, policy-makers will tend to cause inflation rates that are above the socially optimal level, a phenomenon referred to as *inflation bias*.

13.3.1   Basic assumptions

Let us assume a Lucas supply function of the same kind as in Chapter 10,

$$y = \bar{y} + b(\pi - \pi^e) \tag{13.1}$$

where y is actual output (in logarithmic form), $\bar{y}$ is the natural rate of output (long-run aggregate supply), π and π^e are actual and expected inflation as before, and $b > 0$ is a parameter capturing the sensitivity of output to deviations in the inflation rate. Central banks (or policy-makers more generally) are assumed to be in control of the actual level of inflation π, whereas the public forms rational expectations about inflation π^e. One might think of these expectations as being manifested in wage contracts so that there is an element of stickiness in inflationary expectations. The only way that central banks can increase output from its natural level $\bar{y}$ is to surprise the public by setting an inflation rate $\pi > \pi^e$.

Let us further assume that central banks are governed in their decision-making by a (dis)utility or social loss function

$$V = \frac{1}{2}(y - y^*)^2 + \frac{1}{2}a(\pi - \pi^*)^2 \tag{13.2}$$

The aim of the central bank is to conduct a monetary policy that ensures that actual output and inflation are as close as possible to some target levels y^* and π^*. $a > 0$ reflects the relative weight given to fighting inflation. Most central banks have inflation fighting as their primary objective, implying $a > 1$. Furthermore, central banks as well as governments will typically want to maintain levels of output (unemployment) that are higher (lower) than the natural rate, i.e. $y^* > \bar{y}$. Let us think of y^* as the level of output associated with full employment. We assume, for simplicity, that the targeted rate of inflation is $\pi^* = 0$.[3]

There are at least two main monetary policy strategies that central banks can follow: either to make *binding inflation commitments* that are independent of the public's expectations or to allow for a *discretionary monetary policy* that takes the public's expectations into account in its decision-making.

If the central bank makes binding commitments, it will not allow itself to adjust levels of inflation as a response to how the economy performs. Assume that the central bank makes a commitment that, no matter what, it will maintain inflation at $\pi = 0$. If the public considers this to be a credible commitment, its inflation expectations will be $\pi^e = 0$. In this case, the central bank will simply set $\pi = 0$, which is the socially optimal level.

13.3.2   Discretionary monetary policy

If the central bank follows a discretionary monetary policy, then its governors allow themselves flexibility by determining the inflation rate after the public has formed its expectations. An important component is further that central banks recognize that actual output is given by (13.1). There is thus a possibility of boosting output by setting an inflation rate above the expected one, as implied by the Lucas supply function. Combing these assumptions gives us the following minimization problem for the central bank:

$$\min_{\pi} V(\pi) = \frac{1}{2}[\bar{y} + b(\pi - \pi^e) - y^*]^2 + \frac{1}{2}a\pi^2 \tag{13.3}$$

However, the public does not want to be fooled, and forms rational expectations about the central bank's inflation policy. Formally, the objective of the public might be described as being aimed at minimizing $(\pi^e - \pi)^2$. In Kydland and Prescott's model, the interaction between the central bank and the public takes the form of a sequential, complete information game where the public moves first by forming π^e, whereupon the central bank sets π conditional on the observed level of π^e.

As usual in sequential games, we find the solution through backward induction, i.e. by starting in the second stage.

Second stage: *The central bank chooses the π that minimizes* (13.3), *taking π^e as given.*

In order to find the level that minimizes (13.3), we need the first-order condition[4]

$$\frac{\partial V}{\partial \pi} = [\bar{y} + b(\pi - \pi^e) - y^*]b + a\pi = 0$$

After some manipulations, the combined levels of π and π^e that satisfy this first-order condition give us the central bank's *best response* (or *reaction*) *function*

$$\pi^r(\pi^e) = \frac{b}{a+b^2}(y^* - \bar{y}) + \frac{b^2\pi^e}{a+b^2} \tag{13.4}$$

where π^r is the level of π that minimizes (13.3).

The reaction function in (13.4), which is graphically illustrated in Figure 13.1, shows two important things. Firstly, the chosen level of π will always be larger than zero since the first term $b(y^* - \bar{y})/(a+b^2) > 0$. The size of this effect depends in turn on the deviation of the socially optimal level of output (and unemployment) y^* from the natural level $\bar{y}$. This is the origin of the *inflation bias* in discretionary monetary policy referred to earlier. Secondly, the central bank's optimal level of inflation will increase linearly with the public's inflation expectations π^e.

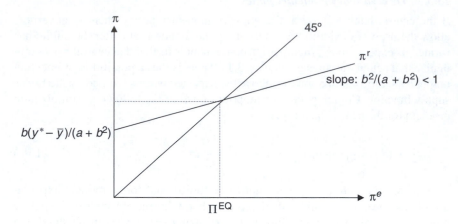

Figure 13.1 Equilibrium inflation under discretionary monetary policy.

In order to obtain the full solution to the model, we need now to move to the first stage:

First stage: *The public forms inflation expectations π^e, taking into account the known response function of the central bank.*

The public knows the rules of the game and realizes that the central bank will attempt to surprise it by setting an inflation higher than the expected one according to (13.4). Since the people want to minimize surprises, they will increase their inflationary expectations until $\pi^e = \pi^r$. Since the slope of the reaction function in (π, π^e) space is smaller than unity, there must be a level where this equality holds. As shown in Figure 13.1, this happens at a level $\pi = \pi^{EQ}$. Inserting $\pi^{EQ} = \pi^e = \pi^r$ into (13.4) and solving gives us the *subgame perfect Nash equilibrium* level of inflation:

$$\pi^{EQ} = \frac{b}{a}(y^* - \bar{y}) > 0$$

The central insight from this expression is, once again, that $\pi^{EQ} > 0$, i.e., even though the official inflation target is $\pi^* = 0$, the fact that discretionary monetary policy is allowed will always give us an inflation rate that is higher than the socially optimal level. The reason is that a target of $\pi^* = 0$ is *time-inconsistent*: when the public's inflation expectations are set first, it is always optimal for the central bank to set $\pi > 0$ in the next stage. Hence, although discretionary policy is more flexible, which sounds like a good thing, it produces inflation rates that are higher than those that would prevail under binding inflation targets.

Note also that since $\pi^{EQ} = \pi^e$ in equilibrium, $y^{EQ} = \bar{y} + b(\pi^{EQ} - \pi^e) = \bar{y}$, i.e. the equilibrium level of output will remain at the natural rate of output and below the socially optimal level y^*. In this sense, the net result of discretionary monetary policy is only a socially suboptimal level of inflation.

13.3.3 Random output shocks

In reality, monetary policy is conducted in a world of genuine uncertainty about how the economy will evolve. As the real business cycle literature has shown, there are good reasons to believe that shocks tend to appear randomly. Furthermore, it is often the case that monetary policy is set partly in response to the realization of random shocks and after the public has formed its expectations (Alesina and Stella 2010).

In order to illustrate this, let us assume that output at time t is now given by

$$y_t = \bar{y} + b(\pi_t - \pi_t^e + \varepsilon_t) \tag{13.5}$$

where ε_t is a random output shock with an expected value $E_t(\varepsilon_t) = 0$. For simplicity, let us also assume that ε_t can assume the values $\gamma > 0$ in good times and $-\gamma$ in bad times with a probability distribution that satisfies $E_t(\varepsilon_t) = 0$.

If we set up the same loss function as before with this new assumption, it will be

$$\min_\pi V(\pi) = \frac{1}{2}[\bar{y} + b(\pi - \pi^e + \varepsilon_t) - y^*]^2 + \frac{1}{2}a\pi^2 \tag{13.6}$$

From the first-order conditions, we can deduce that the central bank's reaction function will now be

$$\pi^r(\pi^e) = \frac{b}{a+b^2}(y^* - \bar{y}) + \frac{b^2(\pi^e - \varepsilon_t)}{a+b^2} \tag{13.7}$$

In the second stage, when the central bank determines the level of inflation by taking the public's expectations π^e as given, it also has information on the actual realization of ε_t. The public, however, will make its expectations before knowing what actually happens to the economy. Their rational expectation about the shock is simply $E_t(\varepsilon_t) = 0$.

When we insert $\pi^{EQ} = \pi^e$ into the expression above as before, we can solve for the equilibrium level of inflation under discretion and uncertainty:

$$\pi^{EQ} = \frac{b}{a+b^2}(y^* - \bar{y}) + \frac{b^2(\pi^{EQ} - \varepsilon_t)}{a+b^2}$$

$$\pi^{EQ}\left(1 - \frac{b^2}{a+b^2}\right) = \pi^{EQ}\left(\frac{a}{a+b^2}\right) = \frac{b}{a+b^2}(y^* - \bar{y}) - \frac{b^2\varepsilon_t}{a+b^2}$$

$$\pi^{EQ} = \frac{b}{a}(y^* - \bar{y}) - b^2\varepsilon_t$$

What this means is that equilibrium inflation will be $\frac{b}{a}(y^* - \bar{y}) - b^2\gamma$ in good times and $\frac{b}{a}(y^* - \bar{y}) + b^2\gamma$ in bad times. Inflation will thus be higher in bad times.

The logic behind this result is that output will be even further away from the target level y^* in such periods, which will make an inflationary policy that boosts output even more tempting for the central bank. The reverse logic applies for good times.

13.3.4 Solutions to time inconsistency

Two types of remedies to time inconsistency are often discussed in the literature: *reputation* and *delegation*. Starting with reputation, this solution depends completely on whether the monetary authority is in place more than one period. If it is not, then it is always optimal to play a nonrepeated game as above. If, however, the policy-maker is in charge for more than one period, expectations about inflation in the second period will depend on actual inflation in the first period. In this case, there will be an intertemporal "externality" of the first-period choice of inflation and policy-makers will in general be less inclined to tolerate high first-period inflation. Reputational considerations should thus at least lead to a lower level of first-period inflation.

A second potential solution to time inconsistency is delegation of monetary authority to an independent central bank that is required (often by law) to focus on fighting inflation. In terms of equation (13.2) in our sequential game setting above, this would be equivalent to handing over authority to some "conservative" central banker who has an $a' > a$ (Rogoff and Sibert 1985). In that case, the intercept in Figure 13.1 would be lower and the slope flatter, which of course would imply an equilibrium level of inflation that is lower than before. It would, however, still be above zero as long as $y^* - \bar{y} > 0$.

13.4 Political business cycles

In the models above, there was no question about what were the socially optimal levels of inflation and output. In Western democracies, economic policy is typically a key issue in elections, and parties often differ in their stated objectives. In the literature on partisan business cycles, pioneered by Hibbs (1977), it is argued that left-wing parties tend to be more concerned about unemployment whereas right-wing parties care more about bringing down inflation.

Such assumptions can be easily incorporated into the basic model.[5] An implicit assumption in this section is that political parties in government can actually influence monetary policy in a discretionary manner.[6] Let the left-wing and right-wing parties have loss functions given by

$$V^L = \frac{1}{2}(y - y^*)^2 + \frac{1}{2}a_L\pi^2$$

$$V^R = \frac{1}{2}(y - y^*)^2 + \frac{1}{2}a_R\pi^2$$

respectively, where V^L is the loss function of the left-wing party and V^R the equivalent function for the right-wing party. The key difference between the two is that $a_R > a_L$, i.e. the right-wing party attaches a relatively higher weight to fighting inflation. Both parties want to achieve full employment, so that $y = y^*$, but the left-wing parties are, as will be demonstrated, more willing to pay a price for this in terms of higher inflation. Compared with the above, let us now set $b = 1$ for simplicity so that output responds fully to a surprise inflation.

If we minimize the loss functions and take the first-order conditions in the usual way, we can derive the optimal response functions

$$\pi^{r,L} = \frac{y^* - \bar{y}}{1 + a_L} + \frac{\pi^e}{1 + a_L} \tag{13.8}$$

$$\pi^{r,R} = \frac{y^* - \bar{y}}{1 + a_R} + \frac{\pi^e}{1 + a_R}$$

and the equilibrium levels of inflation

$$\pi^{EQ,L} = \frac{(y^* - \bar{y})}{a_L} > 0, \quad \pi^{EQ,R} = \frac{(y^* - \bar{y})}{a_R} > 0 \tag{13.9}$$

Since $a_R > a_L$, it follows that $\pi^{EQ,R} < \pi^{EQ,L}$, i.e. equilibrium inflation will be lower when the right-wing party is in power. Note that equilibrium output levels will be $y^L = \bar{y} + \pi^{EQ,L} - \pi^e = \bar{y}$ and $y^R = \bar{y} + \pi^{EQ,R} - \pi^e = \bar{y}$.

In nonelection years, this is well known to the public and they adjust their expectations accordingly. In election years, however, there is an uncertainty about what party will be in power. In line with the discussion about random output shocks above, let us imagine that public expectations are made in the first stage and that the politically controlled central bank then sets the inflation rate after having observed the election result and in accordance with the winning party's preferences.

Let ρ be some objective probability of an election victory for the right-wing party at the time expectations are formed. The probability of a left-wing victory is therefore $1 - \rho$. The expected inflation is then

$$\pi^e = (1 - \rho)\pi^{r,L} + \rho\pi^{r,R}$$

$$= (1 - \rho)\left(\frac{y^* - \bar{y} + \pi^e}{1 + a_L}\right) + \rho\left(\frac{y^* - \bar{y} + \pi^e}{1 + a_R}\right)$$

After some algebra, we can isolate π^e so that it becomes

$$\pi^e = \frac{(y^* - \bar{y})[1 + a_R - \rho(a_R - a_L)]}{(1 + a_R)a_L + \rho(a_R - a_L)} \tag{13.10}$$

This expression implies that π^e will decrease with ρ, the probability of a right-wing election victory. This is well in line with intuition since the right-wing party is more inflation-averse than the left-wing party.

We can insert the result in (13.10) into (13.8) to solve for the actual levels of inflation during an election year t:

$$\pi_t^{EQ,L} = \frac{(y^* - \bar{y})(1 + a_R)}{(1 + a_R)a_L + \rho(a_R - a_L)}$$

$$\pi_t^{EQ,R} = \frac{(y^* - \bar{y})(1 + a_L)}{(1 + a_R)a_L + \rho(a_R - a_L)}$$

Once again, since $a_R > a_L$, it will be the case that $\pi_t^{EQ,L} > \pi_t^{EQ,R}$. Another interesting result emerges if we compare chosen inflation levels by each party during a "mid-term" year when there is no election, and during an election year. Let us imagine that the mid-term year is $t - 1$ and that an election happens the next year at t. Hence, $\pi_{t-1}^{EQ,L}$ is the optimal level of inflation chosen by a left-wing party in office during a mid-term year and is given by (13.9). Let $\pi_{t-1}^{EQ,R}$ be defined in the same way. Then it is easily shown that the following inequalities will hold:

(i) $\pi_t^{EQ,L} < \pi_{t-1}^{EQ,L}$;

(ii) $\pi_t^{EQ,R} > \pi_{t-1}^{EQ,R}$;

(iii) $\pi_t^{EQ,L} > \pi_{t-1}^{EQ,R}$;

(iv) $\pi_t^{EQ,R} < \pi_{t-1}^{EQ,L}$

The direction of the sign in (i) informs us that when a left-wing party is in power and wins the election, inflation will fall during an election year. The reason is that voters give the right-wing party a probability $\rho > 0$ of winning and hence have lower expectations for inflation during the election year. The government-led central bank can thus set a lower level of inflation than before after a left-wing victory. For a right-wing party in power, the reverse logic applies in (ii); in an election year, inflation expectations will rise due to some probability of a left-wing party win and the economy will thus get a higher level of inflation during an election year, even when the right-wing party wins.

Inequalities (iii) and (iv) are perhaps less surprising: if a left-wing party wins the election and takes power from the right-wing party, inflation will increase (iii), whereas if the reverse happens, inflation will fall (iv).

The actual levels of output under different election winners during an election year will be

$$y_t^L = \bar{y} + \pi_t^{EQ,L} - \pi_t^e \tag{13.11}$$

$$= \bar{y} + \frac{\rho(y^* - \bar{y})(a_R - a_L)}{(1 + a_R)a_L + \rho(a_R - a_L)} = \bar{y} + \rho\eta$$

$$y_t^R = \bar{y} + \pi_t^{EQ,R} - \pi_t^e \tag{13.12}$$

$$= \bar{y} - \frac{(1 - \rho)(y^* - \bar{y})((a_R - a_L))}{(1 + a_R)a_L + \rho(a_R - a_L)} = \bar{y} - (1 - \rho)\eta$$

where $\eta > 0$ is given by the cluster of terms in the middle of (13.11) and (13.12). Clearly, it will be the case that $y_t^L > y_t^R$, i.e. with a given pre-election probability of a right-wing election victory ρ, an actual win by the left-wing party will generate a greater level of output than a win by the right-wing party. This is of course only what would be expected given the parties' preferences over economic policy.

However, note that elections will give rise to political business cycles. Output during a mid-term year with no elections and either party in office is just the natural rate $\bar{y}$ since the public correctly anticipates the level of inflation in equilibrium and the central bank therefore cannot boost output by surprising the electorate. But the level in (13.11) is higher than the natural rate during an election year t. The reason is that the public this time anticipated a lower rate of inflation than the one actually chosen by the left-wing party since they gave some probability ρ to a victory by the right-wing party. Hence, the central bank can surprise the electorate with a high inflation and boost output. In case of a right-wing party win, the actual level of inflation will be lower than the one anticipated by the public and output will therefore decline, even if the right-wing party was previously in power. One year after the election, output levels will be back at $\bar{y}$ again.

In Figure 13.2, we show one example of such a political business cycle dynamic. It shows the development of output and inflation when the economy transits from

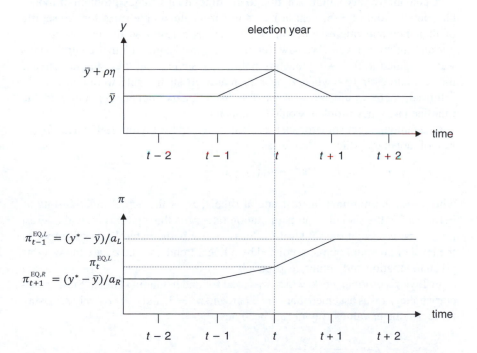

Figure 13.2 Political business cycle effects over time on output (y) and inflation (π) of an unexpected ($\rho > 1/2$) left-wing party election victory over an incumbent right-wing party.

right-wing party rule to an unexpected election victory by the left. In period $t - 1$ and earlier, output and inflation are $\bar{y}$ and $(y^* - \bar{y})/a_R$, respectively. When the election period comes, the probability of a right-wing victory is considered large, $\rho > 1/2$, which is reflected in low inflationary expectations and a relatively low $\pi_t^{EQ,L}$. Due to this surprise, there is a relatively large boom in output, which increases by $\rho\eta > 0$. In period $t + 1$, the economy has settled down at the natural rate of output and the higher equilibrium level of inflation.

The key insight from this section is that even if the same party is in power before and after an election and no fundamentals in the economy have changed, there will still be a temporary cyclic effect on inflation and output that is fully explained by the uncertainty surrounding the election itself.

13.5 The Taylor rule

In practice, central banks do not choose the inflation rate directly. They influence inflation mainly through their determination of the nominal interest rate that other banks in the country are charged when they borrow from the central bank. This rate is usually referred to as the *repo rate*.[7] The central bank repo rate, in turn, influences interest rates in the financial sector as a whole and the rate of price increases in the rest of the economy.

A potentially very simple solution to the time-inconsistency problem of monetary policy would be for central banks to formulate simple rules for the setting of their nominal interest rate (the repo rate) as a response to changes in output and inflation levels. We saw, for instance, in Chapter 11 that central banks were assumed to follow a monetary policy rule saying that they should increase the real interest rate r when Y or π increased. If such a rule were consistently followed, there would be no room for discretionary monetary policy and the time-inconsistency problem would be reduced.

One famous suggestion for such a rule is provided by Taylor (1993). The *Taylor rule* of monetary policy is defined as

$$i_t = \pi_t + r_t^* + a_\pi(\pi_t - \pi^*) + a_y(y_t - \bar{y})$$

where i_t is the nominal interest rate at time t, π_t is the actual inflation rate as before, π^* is the socially optimal inflation rate, r_t^* is the equilibrium real interest rate, y_t is the actual output level (in logs), and $\bar{y}$ is the natural rate of output or the level of potential output predicted by a linear trend. a_π and a_y are the weights given to inflation and output, respectively.

In Taylor's original work, which was used for understanding United States monetary policy, it was assumed that $r_t^* = 2$ percent, $\pi^* = 2$, and $a_\pi = a_y = 1/2$.[8] Using these parameter values, Taylor rule becomes

$$i_t = \pi_t + 2 + \frac{\pi_t - 2}{2} + \frac{y_t - \bar{y}}{2}$$

$$= 1 + \frac{3\pi_t}{2} + \frac{y_t - \bar{y}}{2}$$

Hence, when both output and inflation are at their preferred levels (so that $\pi_t - 2 = y_t - \bar{y} = 0$), then $i_t = 4$ percent. If inflation rises by 1 percent above this level, i.e. $\pi_t = 3$, while the other values remain constant, the rule says central banks should raise their nominal interest rate by 1.5 percent to 5.5 percent. Similarly, if output rose so that it was 1 percent above its long-run trend ($y_t - \bar{y} = 1$), then the nominal interest rate should be raised by 0.5 percent. Taylor (1993) showed that this rule was very close to the actual observed response of the Federal Reserve in the United States to levels and changes in output and inflation.

13.6 Seigniorage

The time-inconsistency problem above is mainly meant to describe the situation in advanced Western economies with benevolent monetary authorities and governments. In countries with weak political institutions and autocratic rulers, it is unlikely that the real objective function of the ruling elite has much in common with the social loss function in the section above. In such countries, the ruling elite often controls monetary authorities and demands money to be printed in order to finance this or that expenditure. This practice, referred to as *seigniorage*, frequently results in *hyperinflation*.[9] This section will analyze the mechanics of seigniorage.

Consider once again the money market equation

$$\frac{M}{P} = L(r + \pi^e, Y)$$

where we assume for simplicity that r and Y are unaffected by the money growth rate and that $\pi = \pi^e$. Also, as in Section 11.2, inflation equals the money growth rate: $\pi = \frac{\dot{M}}{M} = g_m$.

Let us assume that the government now becomes involved in a very costly endeavour for which it cannot easily get financing from the international community, such as a war.[10] The only short-run solution to the financing difficulty is to order the central bank to print money that the government can use to meet its new expenditures. The increase in the nominal money stock from this money printing is $\dot{M}$. If we divide this by the aggregate price level, we get the level of seigniorage S:

$$S = \frac{\dot{M}}{P} = \frac{\dot{M}}{M}\frac{M}{P} = g_m \frac{M}{P} \tag{13.13}$$

The reformulated expression on the right-hand side explains why seigniorage is sometimes referred to as an *inflation tax* on real money balances, where the money growth rate is the "tax" rate.

In a money market equilibrium, it must be the case that $M/P = L(r + \pi^e, Y)$. Inserting this term into (13.13) gives us

$$S = g_m L(r + g_m, Y) \tag{13.14}$$

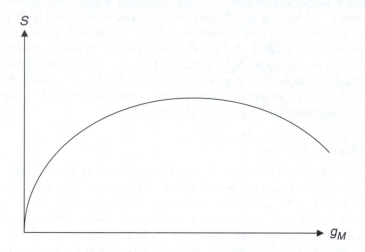

Figure 13.3 The inflation-tax Laffer curve.

The interesting aspect of this expression is that it shows that money printing will have a negative impact on money demand since it will increase the nominal interest rate $i = r + g_m$. There is thus a trade-off: on the one hand, printing more money increases government revenue; on the other hand, it decreases the "tax base" by decreasing the amount of real money balances held in society. Taking derivatives on the basis of (13.14) shows formally the positive and negative effects:

$$\frac{\partial S}{\partial g_m} = \underset{(+)}{L(r + g_m, Y)} + \underset{(-)}{g_m L_i(r + g_m, Y)}$$

Note that the second term approaches zero as g_m goes to zero, whereas $L(r + g_m, Y)$ is positive even if $g_m = 0$. As g_m rises, it is plausible that the second negative term will eventually dominate and make the whole expression negative. In that case, the relationship between S and g_m is shaped like an inverted "U", as shown in Figure 13.3. The curve in Figure 13.3 has been referred to as *the inflation-tax Laffer curve*.[11] A nonbenevolent government should thus create inflation up to the maximum where $\frac{\partial S}{\partial g_m} = 0$.[12] Although this might seem like a cynical type of analysis, it is a well-known fact that hyperinflations are almost always directly caused by governments and that they can be curbed relatively easy if there is a political will to do so.

14 The Open Economy

The models analyzed so far have all assumed a closed economy, i.e. one where trade does not occur. In this final chapter, we will analyze the effects of opening the economy to trade and to capital flows across borders. In reality, total trade (exports plus imports) often amounts to a substantial proportion of GDP, especially in small countries.

In the sections below, we start by defining key concepts and relations such as the current account, the balance of payments, and nominal versus real exchange rates. We then introduce a representative agent framework with a utility-maximizing individual who optimizes a consumption stream in a two-period model. The purpose of this exercise is to show that a balanced current account might not be optimal in all periods. We then discuss more traditional models in the Keynesian tradition of sticky prices such as the Mundell–Fleming model, and the theory of exchange rate overshooting. Finally, we also analyze the criteria for an optimal currency union.

14.1 Open economy accounting

14.1.1 The current account

In the national accounts, total GDP on the user side is written as

$$Y = C + I + G + X - M$$

where $X - M = NX$ represents *net exports*, or the *current account balance*. When $X > M$, so that the country exports more than it imports, we have a current account surplus, whereas $X < M$ implies a current account deficit. A current account surplus means that a country produces more than it uses up domestically, so that $Y > C + I + G$. Such a country might be seen as being a net lender to foreigners, whereas countries with current account deficits are net borrowers from the outside world.

The current account therefore changes the definition of national savings. Let total private savings in an economy be $S^P = Y - C - T$, where T is total taxes, and total public savings is $S^G = T - G$; then total national savings are

$$S = S^P + S^G = Y - C - G = I + NX \tag{14.1}$$

In an open economy, total savings might thus be equal to I, but can depend on net exports.

Equation (14.1) can further be reformulated as

$$NX = S^P - I - (G - T)$$

For a given level of $S^P - I$, a large government budget deficit $G > T$ is most likely associated with a current account deficit $NX < 0$. This scenario, sometimes referred to as *twin deficits*, has characterized the world's largest economy, the United States, during the last decade.

14.1.2 Balance of payments

The balance of payments shows all financial and trade transactions that occur between a country (the *home country*) and the rest of the world. The current account is one part of the balance of payments. The other part is the *capital account*, which measures the net capital and financial flows between the home country and the rest of the world. The capital account is affected positively if foreigners buy assets in the home country (*capital inflow*) and negatively if domestic people buy assets abroad (*capital outflow*). By construction, we must have that

$$\text{Balance of payments} = \text{Current account} + \text{Capital account} = 0$$

Hence, a current account deficit, i.e. a situation where $NX = X - M < 0$, must be balanced by a capital account surplus, i.e. that foreigners buy capital assets in the home country to an extent such as the capital inflow exceeds the capital outflow. The assets in questions are often financial assets like bonds. Hence, current account deficits are typically financed by international net borrowing (selling government bonds to foreigners), whereas a surplus would imply the opposite.

Let us denote a country's net stock of accumulated foreign financial assets at some year t to be B_t. The current account can then be described as

$$NX_t = B_{t+1} - B_t = Y_t + r_t B_t - C_t - I_t - G_t \tag{14.2}$$

If $NX_t > 0$, then $B_{t+1} > B_t$ and the economy's stock of foreign assets increases. If we think of B_t as bonds, then the country is "paid" with foreign bonds to make up for the difference between exports and imports with the rest of the world. If instead imports exceed exports, so that $NX_t < 0$, then the country needs to borrow in order to import more than they export. In this case, the stock of foreign assets decrease. The existing stock of foreign bonds at time t, B_t, earns an interest return of r_t.[1]

14.1.3 Exchange rates

The nominal exchange rate e shows the price of a unit of foreign currency in terms of the home-country currency.[2] A rise in the exchange rate thus means that the foreign currency becomes more expensive, which means a weakening, or *depreciation*, of the home currency. In an analogous manner, should e fall, that would imply a strengthening, or *appreciation*, of the home currency compared with the specific foreign currency in question.

Let the aggregate price level in the foreign country be P^f and the aggregate price level in the home country P, as before. Then the real exchange rate is defined as

$$\epsilon = \frac{e P^f}{P}$$

For example, consider a comparison between the Swedish krona and the euro. The nominal exchange rate is roughly 10 (1 euro costs 10 kronor), whereas the price level is perhaps 5 percent higher in the euro zone, on average. In that case, the real euro/krona exchange rate will be $10 \cdot 1.05 = 10.5$.

A rising real exchange rate, i.e. a depreciation, means that foreign goods and services are becoming more expensive relative to those produced in the home country. Hence, consumers in the home country will likely substitute more expensive foreign goods for cheaper home-produced goods. This will imply that net exports rise, i.e. exports from the home country increase and imports decrease. This relationship is an outcome of a more complicated theoretical exercise called the Marshall–Lerner condition.[3]

14.2 A representative agent framework

So far, we have not said anything about the choices countries make regarding levels and dynamics of the current account, etc. In order to do that, we need to introduce micro foundations, i.e. assume something about the preferences of a typical citizen.

Let us consider a simple two-period model where a representative individual maximizes the utility function

$$U = u(c_1) + \beta u(c_2)$$

where $c_t \geq 0$ is individual consumption.[4] The function has the usual properties of $u'(c_t) > 0$, $u''(c_t) < 0$, and $\beta \leq 1$.

For the economy as a whole, the current account follows the basic dynamics as described in (14.2). The investment equation is given by $I_t = K_{t+1} - K_t$, where K_t is the capital stock at time t. We assume for simplicity that capital depreciation is zero. Rearranging the capital account expression in (14.2) and using the expressions for I_t, the change in total domestic wealth can be written as

$$B_{t+1} + K_{t+1} - (B_t + K_t) = Y_t + r_t B_t - C_t - G_t = S_t \tag{14.3}$$

where S_t is total national savings, Y_t is total output, $r_t B_t$ is net return on holding foreign assets, C_t is aggregate consumption, and G_t is government spending. Hence, total savings in this economy can be used for either domestic capital or accumulating foreign financial assets.

Individuals start off with some capital endowment $K_1 > 0$. In our two-period setting with selfish individuals who have no preference for leaving anything to a future generation, we will assume that $K_3 = 0$. Hence, $I_2 = K_3 - K_2 = -K_2$. Furthermore, we will have that $B_1 = B_3 = 0$, i.e. the economy starts without any foreign assets and also ends without any. For simplicity, we imagine that the economy has only one (representative) individual, so that $c_t = C_t$. Output is produced by using capital according to a standard production function $Y_t = F(K_t)$ where $F'(K_t) > 0$ and $F''(K_t) < 0$.

The current account equation (14.2) and the assumptions just mentioned imply that

$$B_2 = Y_1 - C_1 - I_1 - G_1 = F(K_1) - C_1 - (K_2 - K_1) - G_1$$

Inserting the assumed parameter values for $t = 2$ into (14.3) gives us

$$B_3 + K_3 - B_2 - K_2 = -B_2 - K_2 = F(K_2) + r B_2 - C_2 - G_2$$

The intuition for the latter expression is simply that second-period consumption will partly come from having sold off or "eaten" the capital and assets stocks B_2 and K_2. If we isolate B_2 in the equations above and combine them, we can get an expression that implicitly defines the intertemporal budget constraint for a representatitive individual in the economy:

$$F(K_1) - C_1 - (K_2 - K_1) - G_1 = \frac{C_2 + G_2 - K_2 - F(K_2)}{(1 + r_2)}$$

$$F(K_1) - G_1 + \frac{F(K_2) - G_2}{(1 + r)} = C_1 + K_2 - K_1 + \frac{C_2 - K_2}{(1 + r)}$$

By using this constraint, we can set up the representative agent's Lagrange optimization problem as

$$\Gamma = u(C_1) + \beta u(C_2)$$

$$+ \lambda \left(F(K_1) - G_1 + \frac{F(K_2) - G_2}{1 + r} - C_1 - K_2 + K_1 + \frac{K_2 - C_2}{1 + r} \right)$$

where we want to find the levels of C_1, C_2, and K_2 that maximize utility.

The first-order conditions are

$$\frac{\partial \Gamma}{\partial C_1} = u'(C_1^*) - \lambda = 0$$

$$\frac{\partial \Gamma}{\partial C_2} = \beta u'(C_2^*) - \frac{\lambda}{1+r} = 0$$

$$\frac{\partial \Gamma}{\partial K_2} = \lambda \left(\frac{F'(K_2^*)}{1+r} - 1 + \frac{1}{1+r} \right) = 0$$

The first two conditions can easily be combined to obtain the usual Euler equation result that, optimally, $u'(C_1^*) = \beta(1+r)u'(C_2^*)$. Rearranging the last condition gives the equally familiar result that $F'(K_2^*) = r$, i.e. investments should be made up to the point where the marginal product of capital equals the marginal cost r.

Without further simplifications, the first-order conditions cannot be used for finding explicit solutions. Let us therefore assume that $\beta(1+r) = 1$, which implies that we get the consumption smoothing result of $C_1^* = C_2^* = C^*$. Inserting this solution back into the intertemporal budget constraint gives us

$$C^* = \frac{(Y_1 + K_1 - G_1)(1+r) + F(K_2^*) - G_2 - rK_2^*}{2+r}$$

Optimal consumption thus increases with Y_1 and K_1 and is crowded out by government spending G_1 and G_2.

Since we have now identified the optimal consumption path, we can also define the optimal first-period current account level to be

$$NX_1^* = B_2^* = Y_1 - C^* - I_1 - G_1 \tag{14.4}$$

$$= Y_1 - \frac{(Y_1 + K_1 - G_1)(1+r) + F(K_2^*) - G_2 - rK_2^*}{2+r}$$

$$- (K_2^* - K_1) - G_1$$

Note that we allow for the case that $B_2 < 0$, which would imply a current account deficit and that the country is a net lender in the first period on the international market. In the second period, we have ruled out the possibility that the country ends with either debts or positive assets, so $NX_2^* = B_3 - B_2^* = -B_2^* = -NX_1^*$. Hence, if there is a current account surplus in the first period ($B_2^* > 0$), there must an equivalent deficit in the next (and last) period, and vice versa. What we are analyzing is therefore only the dynamics of the current account, not its "final" level.

To start with, a current account surplus ($B_2 > 0$) is more likely if initial capital and income K_1 and $Y_1 = F(K_1)$ are high. The derivative with respect to K_1 is $\partial NX_1^* / \partial K_1 = [F'(K_1) + 1]/(2+r) > 0$, which is clearly positive. Hence, countries that are initially rich in capital are likely to "choose" a current account surplus in the first period, i.e. to export more than they import. The intuition for this surplus in national saving is really the same as in the permanent income model of consumption: since individuals aim to smoothe consumption, they will save when incomes are abnormally high and use up the savings when incomes are lower.

How about the pattern of government spending, G_1 and G_2? First, note that if $G_1 = G_2 = \bar{G}$, then $\partial NX_1^*/\partial \bar{G} = 0$. The reason is that an increase in $\bar{G}$ would decrease C^* by exactly the same amount and the two effects in (14.4) would cancel each other out. If, however, it was known for instance that the government would decrease only G_2 while keeping G_1 constant, then we find from the derivative that $\partial NX_1^*/\partial G_2 = 1/(2 + r) > 0$, i.e. a decrease in G_2 should cause a current account deficit in the first period. The intuition is that a decrease in G_2 would cause optimal consumption C^* to rise in (14.4) while holding all other variables constant.

14.3   The Mundell–Fleming model

Open economy issues are also frequently analyzed in a Keynesian setting without micro foundations. The Mundell–Fleming model, associated with economists Robert Mundell and Marcus Fleming, introduces a balance of payments equation into the standard IS–LM framework. The current account, or net exports, part of the balance of payments equation can be written as a function

$$X - M = NX(\epsilon, Y, Y^f)$$

where ϵ is the real exchange rate, Y is home-country aggregate income, and Y^f is the income of the rest of the world.[5] As already mentioned, NX should increase with ϵ since foreign goods will then become relatively more expensive and boost exports. NX should, however, fall with domestic income Y since a higher income means that people spend more on imported goods. Analogously, if the foreign income level increases, foreign demand for home-country goods will increase so that exports are boosted, which leads to a rise in NX.

Assuming an open economy changes the nature of planned expenditures that make up the IS equation. Equilibrium on the goods market now requires that

$$Y = E(Y, r, G, \epsilon, Y^f)$$

where ϵ and Y^f are included since they influence the current account. The IS curve will actually be flatter in the open economy scenario because national income Y has both a positive effect through increased consumption and a negative effect through the impact on imports.

Rather than an MP curve, let us now work with a traditional *LM curve*. Whereas an MP curve includes a monetary policy rule $r(Y, \pi)$ whereby the central bank's interest rate reacts to changes in income levels and inflation, we now simply assume

$$\frac{M}{P} = L(r, Y)$$

As will be shown below, r might respond to the balance of payments situation. Monetary policy instead enters as changes in real money supply M/P. In this model, we are not primarily interested in inflation and will assume $\pi^e = 0$ for simplicity so that the nominal interest rate $i = r + \pi^e$ equals the real one, $i = r$. We will indeed assume throughout this section the aggregate price level P is sticky in the short run.

As before, we have that $L_r < 0$ and that $L_Y > 0$. Hence, an increase in Y will increase money demand. In order to preserve the money market equilibrium, we must have that r increases so that money demand falls back again to equal M/P. The LM curve will thus feature a positive association between r and Y.

The balance of payments equation is given by the current account plus the capital account. The level of the capital account, CA, depends primarily on the real interest differential between the home country and the rest of the world $r - r^f$. There are two main scenarios for how the nominal interest rate differential will matter. In the first scenario with *perfect capital mobility* between countries, there can be no interest rate difference, i.e. $r = r^f$. If there is *imperfect capital mobility*, perhaps due to regulations in the international capital market, then r and r^f need not be exactly identical. In that case, the current account will generally be a function of the interest rate differential $CA(r - r^f)$, where

$$\frac{\partial CA(r - r^f)}{\partial (r - r^f)} = CA_{r - r^f} > 0$$

This means that capital will flow into the country if the interest rate domestically, r, is larger than that abroad, r^f.

The current account and capital account equations taken together define the balance of payments (BOP) curve:

$$NX(\epsilon, Y, Y^f) + CA(r - r^f) = 0$$

In the case of perfect capital mobility, the BOP curve will be horizontal at $r = r^f$. With imperfect capital mobility, the BOP curve will be upward-sloping. To see why, consider an increase in Y. Such an increase means that imports rise, which leads to a fall in NX. In order to preserve the balance of payments "balanced" at zero, this requires an offsetting rise in the capital account. Such a rise can only come about through an increase in the domestic interest rate r. When the interest rate rises, capital will flow into the country to finance to current account deficit. Another implication is that there will be a positive association between r and Y.

We are now equipped with three curves: the IS curve (with net exports), the LM curve, and the BOP curve. The curves form a flexible and useful framework for understanding the effect of fiscal and monetary policy in an open economy setting.

Many different scenarios may be analyzed. For instance, let us consider the case of perfect capital mobility, fixed exchange rates, and an expansive monetary policy, as shown in Figure 14.1. The economy is initially in an equilibrium where all curves cross. An increase in the nominal money stock (with prices staying

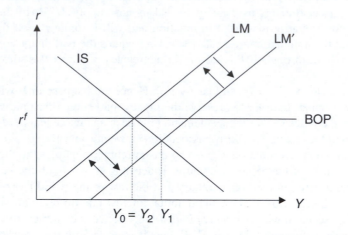

Figure 14.1 Expansionary monetary policy with fixed exchange rates and perfect capital mobility.

constant) leads to a shift in the LM curve to the right. This will cause a fall in the real interest rate below the international level r^f. As a result, people will want to buy foreign bonds and there will be a large capital outflow. Since the exchange rate is supposed to be fixed, the central bank needs to purchase domestic currency in order to keep it at its fixed level. This leads to a reduction in nominal money supply, and the LM curve shifts back again to its initial position Y_0. In other words, under perfect capital mobility and a fixed exchange rate, monetary policy will be ineffective.

Let us now consider a quite different scenario with imperfect capital mobility, fixed exchange rates, and a fiscal expansion. In this case, the BOP curve is upward-sloping, as shown in Figure 14.2. The expansionary fiscal policy (increase in G) causes the IS curve to shift to the right. This causes the interest rate to rise, which in turn implies large capital inflows, i.e. foreign people buy domestic government bonds. This puts pressure on the exchange rate to appreciate (ϵ falls). In order to keep the fixed exchange rate, the central bank must increase money supply, which shifts the LM curve to the right. The end result is an increase in income from Y_0 to Y_2, as shown in the figure. Fiscal policy will thus be relatively effective under these circumstances, but it would have been even more effective if there had been perfect capital mobility.

14.4   Exchange rate overshooting

In the Mundell–Fleming model above, prices did not adjust in the short run and expectations about exchange rate movements did not play any role. The model by

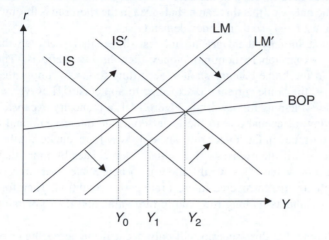

Figure 14.2 Expansionary fiscal policy with fixed exchange rates and imperfect capital mobility.

Dornbusch (1976) shows that when expectations are taken into account under flexible exchange rates, there might be *overshooting* in the adjustment of the exchange rate which makes these extra volatile.

The model builds on two key premises. The first is that real interest rate differentials between the home country and the rest of the world should be explained by the following expression:

$$r_t = r^f + E_t(e_{t+1} - e_t) \tag{14.5}$$

The home-country nominal interest rate at time t should be equal to the interest rate abroad r^f plus the expected change in the exchange rate between $t+1$ and t. Should we, for instance, observe that $r_t > r^f$, then it must be the case that the home currency is expected to depreciate so that $E_t(e_{t+1} - e_t) > 0$.[6] Relation (14.5) shows the equality that must prevail if an investor is going to be indifferent about investing a certain amount of money either in the home currency or in the foreign currency and is often referred to as the *uncovered interest rate parity*.

The other basic premise is the standard expression for equilibrium in the money market:

$$\frac{M}{P} = L(r_t, Y_t)$$

The price level P is assumed to adjust only slowly, as in most Keynesian models.

To illustrate the main implications of the model, consider an expansionary monetary policy from the central bank at time t that increases nominal money supply M. With prices held constant in the short run, this means that real money supply increases. The only way that this can be balanced in the short run is through a fall in the real interest rate r_t so that money demand rises.

Let us assume that initially there are no interest differentials between the two countries. The expansion in nominal money then has two effects. The lower interest rate in the home country should, according to (14.5), imply that $E_t(e_{t+1} - e_t) < 0$, i.e. the home currency is expected to appreciate. However, as shown in the Mundell–Fleming framework in Figure 14.1, a monetary expansion will lead to an outflow of capital due to the lower domestic interest rate and a depreciation of the currency in the longer run. The only way to reconcile equilibria in the two markets is if the exchange rate initially depreciates by more than its long-run equilibrium value. This would allow it to appreciate over time so that it eventually satisfies the uncovered interest rate parity condition. Therefore the exchange rate overshoots its long-run equilibrium value and then gradually appreciates.

It is important to note that this scenario will only occur if the aggregate price level is sticky. It will not happen if prices immediately adjust to the increase in money supply.

14.5 Currency unions

There are numerous currencies in the world. Some have been created very recently, such as the euro, whereas others have a very long history. Are the borders of one country always the natural boundary also for a currency? Since the newly created euro area includes 17 countries, that question must be answered negatively. But what, then, are the determinants of an optimally balanced currency area? Would it be optimal if the whole world had the same currency?

In a famous early article, Mundell (1961) spelled out the necessary criteria for a successful currency union:

- *Labor mobility and an integrated labor market.* If this is not the case, workers will remain in depressed regions and expanding regions will be constrained by lack of access to labor.
- *Capital mobility* and *price and wage flexibility.*
- A *common risk sharing mechanism* so that adversely affected regions are supported by the more fortunate ones. This might, for instance, take the form of income redistribution of tax revenues.
- The regions included should have *similar business cycles.* If certain regions have cycles that are very asymmetric compared with the majority of regions, the adversely affected regions might have benefited from depreciation but are unable to carry out any with a joint currency.

The literature in this area has recently been primarily concerned with the euro area. Recent events during 2010 appear to confirm that certain countries (such as Greece) clearly do not fit some of Mundell's requirements very well. In general, capital mobility across Europe is fairly good but labor mobility is still not substantial. A common risk sharing mechanism is perhaps about to be created, but it is doubtful whether the euro countries typically face symmetric shocks. Apart from the economic criteria cited above, there might of course also be political reasons why countries choose to form currency unions.

15 Mathematical Appendix

15.1 Introduction

This book requires that the student be familiar with certain tools of differential calculus. Fortunately, it is sufficient to limit our analysis to functions of one variable. The following concepts are discussed:

- derivatives of some basic functions
- simple differentiation rules
- chain differentiation
- implicit function differentiation
- applications to macroeconomics

The material of the appendix is rather standard. More detailed presentations can be found in most first-year calculus textbooks.

15.2 Derivatives of some basic functions

Consider a real-valued function $f(x)$ where $x \in \mathbb{R}$. The derivative of f at some point x_0, which is denoted by $f'(x_0)$ or $\frac{df(x)}{dx}\big|_{x=x_0}$, is equal to the change in the value of f if one infinitesimally changes x_0. That is,

$$f'(x_0) = \lim_{x \to x_0} \frac{f(x) - f(x_0)}{x - x_0} \tag{15.1}$$

A function is called *differentiable* at x_0 if this limit exists.

Since on many occasions it could be quite troublesome to calculate such a limit, a number of rules allow us to do so without actually having to use the formal definition of the derivative.

Constant function: $f(x) = c$
The derivative of the constant function is

$$f'(x) = 0 \quad \forall x \in \mathbb{R} \tag{15.2}$$

Identity function: $f(x) = x$

$$f'(x) = 1 \quad \forall x \in \mathbb{R} \tag{15.3}$$

Power: $f(x) = x^n$

The exponent could in principle be any constant n. The derivative of this function is given by

$$f'(x) = nx^{n-1} \quad \forall x \in \mathbb{R} \tag{15.4}$$

Notice that the identity function is a special case of a power with $n = 1$. To verify the previous rule, we substitute $n = 1$ in equation (15.4) and we obtain $f'(x) = x^0 = 1$.

Exponential function: $f(x) = e^x$

The exponential is probably the most important function in calculus. Its base is the irrational number $e \approx 2.7$. It has the very interesting and unique[1] property of being neutral to differentiation. Namely,

$$f'(x) = e^x \quad \forall x \in \mathbb{R} \tag{15.5}$$

Logarithmic function: $f(x) = \ln x$

The natural logarithm ln is the inverse of the exponential function. That is, if, for some arbitrary $x \in \mathbb{R}$, one obtains the value $y = e^x$, then one could go backwards by evaluating the logarithmic function at y, which would yield $\ln y = x$. Notice that the logarithmic function is defined only for positive real numbers. Its derivative is given by the following equation:

$$f'(x) = \frac{1}{x} \quad \forall x \in (0, \infty) \tag{15.6}$$

15.3 Differentiation rules

On many occasions a function has a rather complicated structure, which makes it quite difficult, to calculate its derivative. In order to simplify the differentiation, we apply a number of rules that break the initial function into smaller pieces that can be handled more easily.

15.3.1 Sum of functions

Consider two functions $f_1(x)$ and $f_2(x)$. The derivative of the function $f(x) = f_1(x) + f_2(x)$ is given by the following equation:

$$f'(x) = f_1'(x) + f_2'(x) \tag{15.7}$$

This rule can be generalized to an arbitrary finite sum of functions. Consider, for example, the function $f(x) = x^2 + e^x$. Obviously this is the sum of $f_1(x) = x^2$

and $f_2(x) = e^x$. The derivatives of both f_1 and f_2 can be easily calculated. Therefore the derivative of f would be given by $f(x) = 2x + e^x$.

15.3.2   Multiplication with a scalar

Consider a function g and let the function f be defined as $f(x) = cg(x)$, where $c \in \mathbb{R}$. The derivative of f is given by the following equation:

$$f'(x) = cg'(x) \quad \forall x \in A \tag{15.8}$$

Take, for example, the function $f(x) = 4x^3$. It is easy to see that $f'(x) = 4 \cdot 3x^{3-1} = 12x^2$. Setting $c = -1$ and combining the two rules (sum of functions and multiplication with a scalar) entails a similar rule for the difference $f = f_1 - f_2$, namely, $f'(x) = f_1'(x) - f_2'(x)$.

15.3.3   Product of functions

Consider two functions $f_1(x)$ and $f_2(x)$. The derivative of the function $f(x) = f_1(x)f_2(x)$ is given by the following equation:

$$f'(x) = f_1'(x)f_2(x) + f_1(x)f_2'(x) \tag{15.9}$$

Consider, for example, the function $f(x) = xe^x$. The derivative of f is given by $f'(x) = (x)'e^x + x(e^x)' = e^x + xe^x$.

15.3.4   Division of functions

Consider two functions $f_1(x)$ and $f_2(x)$. The derivative of the function $f(x) = \frac{f_1(x)}{f_2(x)}$ is given by the following equation:

$$f'(x) = \frac{f_1'(x)f_2(x) - f_1(x)f_2'(x)}{[f_2(x)]^2} = \frac{f_1'(x)}{f_2(x)} - \frac{f_1(x)f_2'(x)}{[f_2(x)]^2} \tag{15.10}$$

Notice that the function is defined only for those x that do not make f_2 equal to 0, since otherwise the division would not be defined in the first place. An example of such a function is $f(x) = \frac{x^2+1}{x-1}$, which yields $f'(x) = \frac{2x(x-1)-(x^2+1)}{(x-1)^2} = \frac{x^2-2x-1}{x^2-2x+1}$, for every $x \neq 1$.

15.4   Chain differentiation

All the previous rules involved functions that could be separated into simple ones. However this is not always the case. Take, for instance, the function $h(x) = e^{x^2+1}$. This is a compound function in the sense that h is a function of some other function g, which is a function of x. That is to say, one could set $g(x) = x^2 + 1$ and

$f(y) = e^y$ and by plugging $g(x)$ into y obtain $h(x) = f(g(x)) = e^{g(x)}$. Since g is depends on x and f depends on g, it is straightforward that f depends on x.

Formally, consider two functions $g(x)$ and $f(g(x))$. We define the *compound function* as follows:

$$h(x) = f(g(x)) \tag{15.11}$$

How would we then differentiate $h(x)$ with respect to x? Intuitively, we would like to see how much h would change due to an infinitesimal change in x. A slight change in x would trigger a change in $g(x)$ of the size of the derivative of g. At the same time, changing $g(x)$ would lead to a change in f that depends on g. Thus, the initial change in x has triggered a chain reaction. Through the effect on the intermediate function, it has caused a change in f. The size of this change would be equal to the size of the change in g times the size of the change that g has caused to f. That is,

$$h'(x) = \frac{df(g(x))}{dx} = \frac{df(g(x))}{dg(x)} \frac{dg(x)}{dx} = f'(g(x))g'(x) \tag{15.12}$$

For example, if $h(x) = e^{x^2+1}$ then $h'(x) = 2x e^{x^2+1}$.

15.5 Implicit function differentiation

Consider a function $f(x)$ and assume that its exact formula is not given explicitly. All that is available is a functional relationship of the form $[f(x)]^2 + f(x) - x + 1 = 0$. Since it is not that easy to first solve this equation with respect to $f(x)$ and then differentiate it in x, we proceed by taking the derivative on both sides of the equation, with the use of the chain rule. This gives $2f(x)f'(x) + f'(x) - 1 = 0$, which is linear in $f'(x)$. Hence $f'(x) = \frac{1}{2f(x)+1}$.

15.6 Applications to macroeconomics

The basic task of macroeconomic theory is to study the relationship between certain measures and how they evolve over time. For that reason, we are usually interested in growth rates.

15.6.1 Growth rate of a multiplicative function

Quite often, we have functions of the form

$$Y(t) = X(t)Z(t)$$

To find the growth rate of $Y(t)$, we need to use both the product rule and the chain rule:

$$\frac{dY(t)}{dt}\frac{1}{Y(t)} = \frac{\dot{Y}(t)}{Y(t)} = \frac{\dot{X}(t)Z(t) + X(t)\dot{Z}(t)}{Y(t)}$$

$$= \frac{\dot{X}(t)Z(t) + X(t)\dot{Z}(t)}{X(t)Z(t)} = \frac{\dot{X}(t)}{X(t)} + \frac{\dot{Z}(t)}{Z(t)}$$

15.6.2 *Growth rate as the derivative of the logarithmic function*

Measures like income growth rate or inflation rate embody the concept of relative change. In discrete time, these are usually expressed by a percentage, but since time is continuous we are forced to go to the limit and examine their relative change in an infinitesimally small time interval.

Consider, for instance, a variable $X(t)$ as a function of time. The instantaneous relative change is given by the growth rate of X with respect to time. Denoting the derivative[2] at t by $\dot{X}(t)$, we can write the growth rate as a fraction $\frac{\dot{X}(t)}{X(t)}$.

Remember from the previous sections that the derivative of the logarithmic function is given by $\frac{d(\ln X)}{dX} = \frac{1}{X}$. Then taking the derivative of $\ln X(t)$ with respect to t and applying the chain rule, we obtain

$$\frac{d\ln X(t)}{dt} = \frac{1}{X(t)}\frac{dX(t)}{dt} \qquad (15.13)$$

Using the appropriate notation, we can rewrite (15.13) as follows:

$$\frac{d\ln X(t)}{dt} = \frac{\dot{X}(t)}{X(t)} \qquad (15.14)$$

Thus, the growth rate of $X(t)$ is nothing but the derivative of the logarithmic function.

15.7 Basic properties of exponents and logarithms

15.7.1 *Exponents*

1. $x^0 = 1, \quad x \neq 0$
2. $x^1 = x$
3. $x^n x^m = x^{n+m}$
4. $\frac{x^n}{x^m} = x^{n-m}, \quad x \neq 0$
5. $(x^n)^m = x^{nm}$
6. $(xy)^n = x^n y^n$
7. $\frac{x^n}{y^n} = (\frac{x}{y})^n, \quad y \neq 0$

15.7.2 Logarithms

1. $\ln 1 = 0$
2. $\ln e = 1$
3. $\ln x + \ln y = \ln(xy)$
4. $\ln x - \ln y = \ln(\frac{x}{y})$
5. $\ln(x^c) = c \ln x$
6. $x = e^{\ln x}$

Notes

Preface

1 Any macro model that, for instance, assumes away unemployment (like many DGE models routinely do) seems to have missed something important about how economies work.

1 Introduction

1 GDP does not include the production of intermediate goods or services, nor production on the black market. The market value of public services like health care are further very imprecisely measured in the national accounts.
2 An individual's purchase of a car for personal use counts as consumption in the national accounts, although it might intuitively be seen as an investment.

2 The Malthusian World

1 See Clark (2007) for an extensive discussion of these relationships.
2 It can be shown that the second-order condition for a maximum is also satisfied since $\partial^2 \ln U_t / n_t^2 < 0$.
3 Note also that this expression is qualitatively similar to the population dynamics equation (2.4).
4 In particular, the Fertile Crescent hosted the wild progenitors of goats, pigs, cattle, and horses among the animals, as well as wheat and barley among the plants. Other regions, such as Australia, had no domesticable species and hence remained at Stone-Age level before European contact.
5 In the Fertile Crescent, the transition to agriculture happened around 8500 BC.
6 The existence of such a trade-off was originally suggested by Becker and Lewis (1973).
7 Time spent on providing the basics for one child τ is supposed to be fixed.
8 The only slight complication is that the $e(g_{t+1})$ curve is drawn in (g_t, e_t) space rather than in (e_t, g_t) space. It still satisfies the specific partial derivatives referred to above.

3 The Solow Growth Model

1 We will refer to the long run as being a time horizon that is at least longer than the duration of a typical business cycle of about five years.
2 An *endogenous* variable is one that is explained by the model itself, whereas an *exogenous* variable is one that we take as given and that is not explained by the model.
3 The function usually also includes the level of technological knowledge, $A(t)$. We will introduce $A(t)$ below.
4 This is sometimes expressed by saying that the production function exhibits homogeneity of degree 1.
5 In the overlapping generations model below, we will instead assume discrete rather than continuous time.

6 To check that the system is stable, try a level of k to the left of k^*. At this level, $sf(k)$ will exceed $(\delta + n)k$, so that $\dot{k} > 0$ and we are moved to the right to an increased level of k. The contrary occurs to the right of k^*. Only at k^* will the system reach a stable point.
7 For a similar discussion, see Romer (1994).
8 This feature is sometimes also referred to as "Harrod neutrality". Other assumptions regarding technology are sometimes made, but will not be discussed here.
9 We will discuss the nature of technology further below.

4 Endogenous Growth Theory

1 Remember that for any variable $x(t)$, it will be the case that $\frac{\dot{x}}{x} = \frac{\partial \ln x}{\partial t}$.
2 This section on the product variety model and the next section on the Schumpeterian growth model follow a structure that is similar to the equivalent sections in Barro and Sala-i-Martin (2004).
3 In general, in this type of model, we might view the competitive and monopoly prices $P^* \in \{1, 1/\alpha\}$ as the two extremes in a range of levels of competition.
4 This is clearly a great simplification. In reality, R&D is usually a very risky enterprise that frequently produces no useful results.
5 In most endogenous growth models, T is assumed to be infinite. In reality, patents typically last for about 20 years.
6 Aghion and Howitt (1992) assume that the arrival of new innovations follows a Poisson process. Here we will leave that process undefined.
7 The inclusion of a human capital stock is a slight departure from the model in Acemoglu et al (2003) but in line with their general argument.

5 The Overlapping Generations Model

1 Hence, for instance, $c_{2,t+1}$ is consumption by old individuals during period $t + 1$.
2 This implicitly assumes the presence of perfect financial markets. We will return to this issue below.
3 This intertemporal budget constraint often enters with a "$\leq$" sign so that consumption should not *exceed* lifetime wage incomes. However, since we have ruled out any bequests, the condition will be satisfied with equality.
4 This can be shown mathematically by using l'Hôpital's rule.
5 We could also simply have inserted the expression for $c_{2,t+1}$ in (5.8) into (5.6) and reached the same result by solving for $\partial \Gamma / \partial c_{1,t} = 0$.
6 The famous Ramsey (1928) growth model is usually set in a continuous-time framework and involves dynamic programming. See Barro and Sala-i-Martin (2004) for an extensive treatment of this model.
7 Recall that in the Solow model, we used an expression $\dot{K}_t = sY - \delta K$. The equivalent expression in discrete time would be $K_{t+1} - K_t = sY - \delta K_t$, where sY is total savings in the economy. Total savings in the model shown here is $s_t L$, and we implicitly assume complete depreciation in each period so that $\delta = 1$. Hence, $K_{t+1} = s_t L$.

6 Equilibrium Business Cycles

1 A "representative" firm should be thought of as characterizing the ideal type of firm behavior, just like a representative individual's utility function represents an ideal type of behavior from the viewpoint of economic theory. Needless to say, by no means all firms are perfect profit maximizers in reality.
2 The second-order condition for maximum is fulfilled if the second derivative satisfies $\frac{\partial^2 \Pi}{\partial L_t^2} < 0$, which is indeed true in this case.

3 Aggregate demand for labor will be $\sum_i L^{i,D} = (\frac{(1-\alpha)A_t^{1-\alpha}}{w_t})^{\frac{1}{\alpha}} \sum_i K_t^i = (\frac{(1-\alpha)A_t^{1-\alpha}}{w_t})^{\frac{1}{\alpha}} K_t$, where K_t is the total capital stock in the economy.

4 We might have done formal comparative statics on (6.11) by using the implicit function rule. However, we will stick to a more informal approach here.

7 Financial Crises

1 A famous recent example of an individual failure of a financing institution is of course the collapse of Lehman Brothers in September 2008.

2 Recent examples include Sweden in 1991 and Iceland in 2008. With some exceptions, the financial crisis of 2008 did not turn into a general bank run among traditional banks, mainly because of various lender insurance schemes supported by governments.

3 One might think of the utility function as describing an individual who is impatient with a probability ρ and impatient with a probability $1 - \rho$.

4 Asterisks (*) will henceforth denote socially optimal levels.

5 The calculation involves quite a bit of algebra and is left for the student as an exercise. The full solution is available upon request.

6 As shown by Chang and Velasco (2001), this result will not apply if the debt incurred in period 0 is long-term. Hence, the longer the duration of loans, the less fragile is the system to depositor panics.

8 Consumption and Saving

1 Formally, this result is given by the partial derivative $\frac{\partial C_t}{\partial \tau} = -c_{\mathrm{mpc}} Y_t < 0$, which implies that a decrease in τ will increase C_t.

2 This assumption will be relaxed in a section below.

3 Note that there will be $T + 1$ time periods since we also count period 0.

4 Negative savings implies that the individual either borrows money with future income as collateral, or uses up accumulated savings.

5 Such savings are often compulsory and take the form of funds for retirement.

6 For an overview of empirical regularities regarding lifetime consumption patterns, see Attanasio (1998).

7 Another interesting prediction from the PIH is that an individual's consumption sensitivity to unexpected changes in income should decrease with T, i.e. older people (with a smaller T) should be more prone to immediately spend windfall gains from lotteries, for instance.

8 In older models, it was often assumed that people formed expectations about future incomes, or about economic phenomena in general, mainly on the basis of their observations of past behavior, so-called *adaptive expectations*.

9 For instance, assuming a random variable X_t, $E_t(X_t) = X_t$ since X_t is actually observed at t and no expectations need to be made. Furthermore, the expectation of some constant η simply equals the constant: $E_t(\eta) = \eta$.

10 This first-order, autoregressive random-walk process might be compared with the AR(1) process for technology in the RBC model. In Hall's model, the equivalent of ρ_A is equal to 1 so that the shock is only felt one period ahead.

11 One such change in expectations might, for instance, concern y_2, which has been realized in period 2 but which was still uncertain in period 1. Note that $\sum_{t=2}^{T} E_2(y_t) = y_2 + \sum_{t=3}^{T} E_2(y_t)$.

12 Such a slowly rising level of consumption is actually well in line with empirical studies on the life-cycle hypothesis.

13 The idea that relative consumption should influence individuals in their decision-making goes back at least to Duesenberry (1952).

14 Time-independent utility from consumption means that the marginal utility of C_t is independent of $C_{j \neq t}$. In the setting above, the marginal utility of C_1 will depend on the level of C_2.

9 Investment and Asset Markets

1 In an economy, there are usually also *human capital investments*, for instance through education, and *social capital investments*, which involve bonding with other people for some economic purpose.
2 According to the "accelerator" model, we have that $K_t = \kappa Y_t$, where $\kappa > 0$ is a constant "capital–output ratio". From this relationship, it follows that if Y_t increases by ΔY_t, then K_t will also increase, i.e. there will be investment: $I_t = \kappa \Delta Y_t$.
3 The section below is similar to the analysis in Sørensen and Whitta-Jakobsen (2005, Chapter 15).

10 Unemployment and the Labor Market

1 Recall that labor demand is implicitly derived from the firm's standard first-order condition for profit maximization where the marginal product equals the wage rate.
2 An alternative profit function would be that firms were maximizing expected profits and hence would only choose one level of L_O and w_I based on the expected outcome.
3 The same basic search and matching model more or less also applies to the marriage market.

11 IS–MP, Aggregate Demand, and Aggregate Supply

1 It is sometimes assumed that investment increases with income Y_t, but we do not employ that assumption here.
2 It is assumed that people earn no interest on ordinary bank deposits, only on long-term investments.
3 For instance, European countries in the euro area have laws stipulating that central banks should be conducted with the primary aim of holding inflation low. In Chapter 13, we discuss one such central bank rule – the *Taylor rule* – which has been empirically observed in the United States.
4 In older textbooks, the AD curve is usually drawn in with some price index P on the vertical axis. We will, however, alter this convention here and instead have the change in the price level, i.e. inflation, on the vertical axis.
5 It is questionable how empirically relevant this assumption about an unobservable aggregate price level was in the year 2012.
6 In equilibrium, investment demand (I) will therefore be equal to savings (S), which is the original reason for the acronym IS.
7 Such a reassessment appears to have been one of the reasons for the credit crunch in the United States in 2008.
8 Note that we thus implicitly assume imperfect competition since prices are set above marginal cost.
9 For an overview of this literature, see Romer (1993).

12 Public Finance and Fiscal Policy

1 In the next chapter (Section 13.6), we will specifically study money printing, or *seigniorage*, and the effects that it might have on the economy.
2 See Barro (1989) for an extensive discussion.
3 See Reinhart and Rogoff (2009b) for an account of such historical episodes.

13 Inflation and Monetary Policy

1 Notions of a positive association between the money stock and inflation appear to date back to ancient times and at least to Copernicus in the 1500s.
2 This is sometimes referred to as the *Fisher effect*.
3 π^* is normally around 2 percent in the Western world.
4 The second-order condition for minimum is satisfied since $\partial^2 V/\partial \pi^2 > 0$.
5 The exposition below is inspired by Alesina and Stella (2010).
6 This is formally not possible in the case of fully independent central banks.
7 This is technically speaking the interest rate that is used when central banks conduct open market operations with the rest of the banking system through short-term *repurchase agreements*. We will not discuss how this mechanism works in this text.
8 This is actually close to what also applies in the euro area. The inflation target for the European Central Bank is 2 percent, for instance.
9 A hyperinflation is sometimes defined as being in place if the inflation rate exceeds 50 percent per month. In most hyperinflation events, inflation is much higher.
10 Wars have been a recurring cause of hyperinflations throughout history.
11 The original Laffer curve depicts the inverted "U" relationship between tax revenue and tax rates.
12 Empirical research has shown that the maximum level of S is found at inflation rates of roughly 200–300 percent (Romer 2005).

14 The Open Economy

1 The sum of GDP and net international factor payments $Y_t + r_t B_t$ is defined as the *gross national income*.
2 For example, the USD exchange rate in terms of the Swedish krona (SEK) is roughly 6.50 at the time of writing (September 2011).
3 Formally, the Marshall–Lerner condition shows that $\frac{\partial NX}{\partial \epsilon} > 0$ if the absolute value of the sum of the price elasticities of exports and imports is more than one.
4 The exposition below is similar to that in Obstfeld and Rogoff (1999, Chapter 1).
5 It is convenient to assume that the world consists of only two countries.
6 Countries with weak currencies will thus generally have higher nominal interest rates. We assume that the international interest rate r^f is time-invariant.

15 Mathematical Appendix

1 Actually the whole family of exponential functions $f(x) = ce^x$, $c \in \mathbb{R}$, has this property.
2 In macroeconomics, it is conventional to use this notation.

Bibliography

Acemoglu, D. and D. Autor (2009) Lectures in labor economics. Unpublished teaching material, http://econ-www.mit.edu/faculty/acemoglu/courses, accessed May 10, 2011.

Acemoglu, D., P. Aghion, and F. Zilibotti (2003) Vertical integration and distance to frontier. *Journal of the European Economic Association*, 1(2–3), 630–638.

Acemoglu, D., S. Johnson, and J. Robinson (2005) The rise of Europe: Atlantic trade, institutional change, and economic growth. *American Economic Review*, 95(3), 546–579.

Aghion, P. and P. Howitt (1992) A model of growth through creative destruction. *Econometrica*, 60(March), 323–406.

Alesina, A. and A. Stella (2010) The politics of monetary policy. NBER Working Paper 15856, NBER.

Alesina, R. and G. Tabellini (1990) A positive theory of fiscal deficits and government debt. *Review of Economic Studies*, 57, 403–414.

Ashraf, Q. and O. Galor (2010) Dynamics and stagnation in the Malthusian epoch. *American Economic Review*, forthcoming.

Attanasio, O. (1998) Consumption demand. NBER Working Paper 6466, NBER.

Barro, R.J. (1974) Are government bonds net wealth? *Journal of Political Economy*, 82(November), 1095–1117.

Barro, R.J. (1979) On the determination of the public debt. *Journal of Political Economy*, 87(October), 940–971.

Barro, R.J. (1989) The Ricardian approach to budget deficits. *Journal of Economic Perspectives*, 3(2), 37–54.

Barro, R.J. and X. Sala-i-Martin (2004) *Economic Growth*, 2nd edition. Cambridge, MA: MIT Press.

Becker, G. and H.G. Lewis (1973) On the interaction between the quantity and quality of children. *Journal of Political Economy*, 81(2), 279–288.

Besley, T. and T. Persson (2010) State capacity, conflict, and economic development. *Econometrica*, 78(1), 1–34.

Blanchard, O. (1985) Debt, deficits, and finite horizons. *Journal of Political Economy*, 93(2), 223–247.

Bowman, D., D. Minehart, and M. Rabin (1999) Loss aversion in a consumption-savings model. *Journal of Economic Behavior and Organization*, 38, 155–178.

Branson, W.H. (1989) *Macroeconomic Theory and Policy*, 3rd edition. New York: Harper & Row.

Caballero, R. (1997) Aggregate investment. NBER Working Paper 6264, NBER.

Chang, R. and A. Velasco (2001) A model of financial crises in emerging markets. *Quarterly Journal of Economics*, 116(2), 489–517.

Clark, G. (2007) *A Farewell to Alms*. Princeton, NJ: Princeton University Press.

Diamond, D.W. and P.H. Dybwig (1983) Bank runs, deposit insurance, and liquidity. *Journal of Political Economy*, 91(3), 401–419.

Diamond, J. (1997) *Guns, Germs and Steel: The Fates of Human Societies*. New York: Norton.

Diamond, P. (1965) National debt in a neoclassical growth model. *American Economic Review*, 55(5), 1126–1150.

Diamond, P. (1982) Aggregate demand management in search equilibrium. *Journal of Political Economy*, 90(5), 881–894.

Dornbusch, R. (1976) Expectations and exchange rate dynamics. *Journal of Political Economy*, 84(6), 1161.

Duesenberry, J. (1952) *Income, Saving, and the Theory of Consumer Behavior*. Cambridge, MA: Harvard University Press.

Frederick, S., G. Loewenstein, and T. O'Donoghue (2002) Time discounting and time preference: A critical review. *Journal of Economic Literature*, 40, 351–401.

Friedman, M. (1957) *A Theory of the Consumption Function*. Princeton, NJ: Princeton University Press.

Friedman, M. (1968) The role of monetary policy. *American Economic Review*, 58(March), 1–17.

Gali, J. and M. Gertler (2007) Macroeconomic modeling for monetary policy evaluation. *Journal of Economic Perspectives*, 21(4), 25–46.

Galor, O. and D. Weil (2000) Population, technology and growth: From the Malthusian regime to the demographic transition. *American Economic Review*, 110, 806–828.

Hall, R.E. (1978) Stochastic implications of the life cycle-permanent income hypothesis. *Journal of Political Economy*, 86(6), 971–987.

Hibbs, D.A. (1977) Political parties and macroeconomic policy. *American Political Science Review*, 71(4), 1467–1487.

Jones, C.I. (1995) R&D-based models of endogenous growth. *Journal of Political Economy*, 103(August), 759–784.

Krugman, P. (1988) Financing vs forgiving a debt overhang. *Journal of Development Economics*, 29, 253–268.

Kydland, F. and E. Prescott (1977) Rules rather than discretion: The inconsistency of optimal plans. *Journal of Political Economy*, 85(June), 473–492.

Kydland, F. and E. Prescott (1982) Time to build and aggregate fluctuations. *Econometrica*, 50, 1345–1370.

Laibson, D. (1997) Golden eggs and hyperbolic discounting. *Quarterly Journal of Economics*, 112(2), 443–477.

Lindbeck, A. and D. Snower (1986) Wage setting, unemployment, and insider-outsider relations. *American Economic Review*, 76(2), 235–239.

Long, J.B. and C.I. Plosser (1983) Real business cycles. *Journal of Political Economy*, 91, 39–69.

Lucas, R.E. (1972) Expectations and the neutrality of money. *Journal of Economic Theory*, 4(April), 103–124.

Lucas, R.E. (1973) Some international evidence of output-inflation tradeoffs. *American Economic Review*, 63(3), 326–334.

Malthus, T. (1798) *An Essay on the Principle of Population*. London.

Mankiw, G. (1985) Small menu costs and large business cycles: A macroeconomic model of monopoly. *Quarterly Journal of Economics*, 100(May), 529–539.

Mankiw, G., D. Romer, and D. Weil (1992) A contribution to the empirics of economic growth. *Quarterly Journal of Economics*, 107(2), 407–437.

Mortensen, D. and C. Pissarides (1994) Job creation and job destruction in the theory of unemployment. *Review of Economic Studies*, 61(3), 397–415.

Mundell, R. (1961) A theory of optimum currency areas. *American Economic Review*, 51(4), 657–665.

Obstfeld, M. and K. Rogoff (1999) *Foundations of International Macroeconomics*, Cambridge, MA: MIT Press.

Olsson, O. and D.A. Hibbs (2005) Biogeography and long-run economic development. *European Economic Review*, 49(4), 909–938.

Phelps, A.W. (1968) Money-wage dynamics and labor market equilibrium. *Journal of Political Economy*, 76(July), 678–711.

Phillips, A.W. (1958) The relationship between unemployment and the rate of change of money wages in the united kingdom, 1861–1957. *Economica*, 25(November), 283–299.

Ramsey, F. (1928) A mathematical theory of saving. *Economic Journal*, 38(152), 543–559.

Rebelo, S. (1991) Long-run policy analysis and long-run growth. *Journal of Political Economy*, 96(June), 500–521.

Rebelo, S. (2005) Real business cycle models: Past, present, and future. NBER Working Paper 11401, NBER.

Reinhart, C. and K.S. Rogoff (2009a) The aftermath of financial crises. *American Economic Review: Papers and Proceedings*, 99(2), 466–472.

Reinhart, C. and K.S. Rogoff (2009b) *This Time Is Different? Eight Centuries of Financial Folly*. Princeton, NJ: Princeton University Press.

Rogoff, K. and A. Sibert (1985) The optimal degree of commitment to an intermediate monetary target. *Quarterly Journal of Economics*, 100(4), 1169–1189.

Romer, D. (1993) The new Keynesian synthesis. *Journal of Economic Perspectives*, 7(1), 5–22.

Romer, D. (2005) *Advanced Macroeconomics Macroeconomics*. Boston: McGraw-Hill.

Romer, P. (1986) Increasing returns and long-run growth. *Journal of Political Economy*, 94(October), 1002–1037.

Romer, P. (1990) Endogenous technological change. *Journal of Political Economy*, 98(October), S71–S102.

Romer, P. (1994) The origins of endogenous growth. *Journal of Economic Perspectives*, 8(Winter), 3–22.

Schumpeter, J. (1934) *The Theory of Economic Development* (translated from the German version published in 1912). New York: Oxford University Press.

Shapiro, C. and J.E. Stiglitz (1984) Equilibrium unemployment as a worker discipline device. *American Economic Review*, 74(3), 433–444.

Solow, R. (1956) A contribution to the theory of economic growth. *Quarterly Journal of Economics*, 70(February), 65–94.

Sørensen, P.B. and H.J. Whitta-Jakobsen (2005) *Introducing Advanced Macroeconomics: Growth and Business Cycles*. Maidenhead: McGraw-Hill.

Taylor, J.B. (1993) Discretion versus policy rules in practice. *Carnegie-Rochester Conference Series on Public Policy*, 39, 195–214.

Woodford, M. (2010) Financial intermediation and macroeconomic analysis. *Journal of Economic Perspectives*, 24(4), 21–44.

Index

Please note: page numbers in **bold** refer to figures.

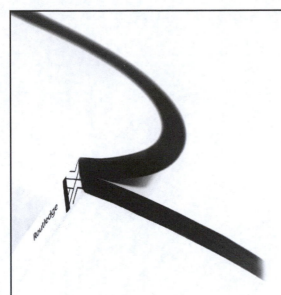

Routledge
Paperbacks Direct

Bringing you the cream of our hardback publishing at paperback prices

This exciting new initiative makes the best of our hardback publishing available in paperback format for authors and individual customers.

Routledge Paperbacks Direct is an ever-evolving programme with new titles being added regularly.

To take a look at the titles available, visit our website.

www.routledgepaperbacksdirect.com

Routledge
Taylor & Francis Group